Spilled Milk

Copyright © 2006

All rights reserved. Printed in the United States of America. No part of this publication may be reproduced, stored in a retrieval system, or transmitted, in any form or by any means electronic, mechanical, photocopying, recording, or otherwise, without the prior written permission of the author.

ISBN 1-58961-521-2
LCCN 2007925173
Published by PageFree Publishing, Inc.
P.O. Box 60
Otsego, Michigan 49078
www.pagefreepublishing.com

Spilled Milk

By

Holly Goldstein

Contents

Acknowledgements ix

Author's Notes xi

Chapter I The Trigger 1

Chapter II Pretty Face 16

Chapter III The Skipper Doll 29

Chapter IV The Clothes Line 42

Chapter V The Refrigerator 62

Chapter VI The Electric Cord 80

Chapter VII Grandma 96

Chapter VIII The Play 114

Chapter IX The Broom 130

Chapter X Scared and Lost — Healing Wounds 143

Dedicated

To the three little girls, who now find healing.

"Lo taamod al dam reakha"

"Thou shalt not stand idle by."
                              Leviticus 19:16

Version of Bible: "The Torah, A Modern Commentary, 1981"

Acknowledgements:

Some say it takes a village to raise a child. I say it's never too late to find the right villages. I have found several villages in my quest for healing. Some of those villages have been in the United States and others in Israel. Unbeknownst to the many who touched my life, I owe tribute to them, for their support and guidance, along with their teachings.

Among the very special people I want to thank most is my friend Pamela. Without her help and teachings I would not be pursuing a Jewish education today. I truly value her friendship, kind heart and patience.

A special thank you to my two sisters, Barbra and Marcia. Without their help, understanding and love, I don't think I would have finished this book. Our relationship has flourished, and real healing has occurred as a result. I will always value and cherish them.

Special thanks to my husband Steve, for his patience, unconditional love, and encouragement. Steve was inspirational and the glue that held me up while working through this daunting process.

My gratitude is extended to my friend Marty, for being a good source of support. And many thanks to my friend Jenny and the countless others I've come in contact with throughout my journey. You have all added to my life.

I cannot express enough appreciation to Lonni at the Catharsis Foundation. Her tenacity and diligence in helping with this project has meant a great deal to me. I'm honored to have her support.

A very special thank you goes to Roberta and Stephanie Gordon for their support and help in this project.

Lastly, I would like to take this opportunity to thank my children. They have shown the most patience and understanding of all. It is because of them I chose to pave a path of healing, and it is because of them the cycle of abuse ended with me.

Author's Notes

Coming to terms with being an abuse survivor takes a great deal of courage. It also takes a great deal of understanding in how a survivor is affected by the abuse he or she has endured. For that purpose, this book was written in three parts. The affects from being abused, the flashbacks of the abuse, and the healing that takes place as a result of the abuse.

The abuse stories in this book are based on the child's life from ages 7 to 18.

This book also depicts the voice and language of a child, young adult, and adult. The vocabulary and tone will reflect the different ages throughout the book.

Please know if you are a survivor of abuse, this book does contain material that could be a trigger or stressor. Therefore, please read with caution.

Some of the names in this book have been changed to protect the privacy of others. This book is based on the true life of the author.

Chapter 1

The Trigger – 1998

"Excuse me," a tall, dark-haired man said as he gently grabbed my waist while briskly walking past me. I'm standing in the entrance of a small town public library. I tightened my grip on the shoulder strap of my black nylon bag, my stomach tensed at his touch. The tall man walked off into an aisle of books; sweat beads formed on my forehead.

I can't remember how old I was when I first began tensing up and flinching at an unexpected touch or sound. My hyper alert startle responses are grafted in my psyche because I suffer from a disorder called PTSD, short for Post Traumatic Stress Disorder. I've suffered from this disorder for as long as I can remember. I developed PTSD early in life; I suppose it was one of my ways of coping, surviving childhood trauma.

I've learned to hide many of my symptoms associated with the abuse, except for the triggers. They come unexpectedly, sometimes during the day and sometimes at night. There are times when I'm triggered somewhere that feels hauntingly familiar, or by an object I've seen that jogs a memory. Certain smells will also trigger a warning response, and then there are times I'll feel danger lurking around me.

There are warnings within my memories. With every memory there are smells, objects of recognition, tastes, sounds, and places that are the clues to the traumatic stories of my past.

Triggers cause flashbacks; pictures or sounds from the past that will flicker into the present. While mini-movies flash in front of me, my mind remembers the scary feelings as my body heads into a tailspin of anxiety.

Just as with the tall man who gently grabbed my waist as he walked past me, my body tenses at the intrusion of an unanticipated stroke, tap, or touch. I remember the fear I feel for tall men; although I don't really know why as it was short men who brought me harm. But, I guess, when I was a little girl, every man was tall.

I'm not a little girl anymore. The trauma is all gone, but my body doesn't know it and my mind refuses to believe it. My head is always in fear while my body feels terrified; one of the many effects of PTSD. The war may have ended in reality, but in the life of an abused brain and body, the battle for finding protection continues.

Scanning the big, quiet library, I took notice of the massive bookcases as my eyes glanced over toward elongated maple desks with their hardwood chairs, and then over to computers stationed behind glass walls. I let out a breath, loosened my grip on the strap of my purse and headed toward the center of the library, passing a few college-aged girls as they studied.

I noticed a brown-haired woman with her hair wrapped in a tight bun at the nape of her neck, standing behind a wood counter. Twirling my dangly Star of David earring, I slowly approached her.

"Excuse me, can I use your microfilm? I want to look up some news articles from the 'Omaha World Herald.'"

"Absolutely! Follow me to these tables," she said, extending one of her arms as if to coach me along with her as she walked out from behind the counter. "I'll show you everything you need to know," the small-framed woman said in high-pitched voice. "Here you go sweetie, you just sit right here, and read these directions, they'll explain how you need to use the machine and insert the microfilm. The ones you're looking for are right over there," she said pointing to a white plastic tower.

"Okay, thank you," elated that she'd taken time to help.

"Now if you need any more help you just come back up to the counter, and I'll help you, okie dokie?" She swiftly walked back to her station as I nodded my head in response.

Placing my purse on the table I looked over at the librarian as she walked back to her counter. *Humm*, I thought as I took a seat on the hard oak chair, *I wonder where she's from? She seems so familiar, what a sad looking flowered dress she's wearing.*

Fumbling through the microfilm, I found the one I was looking for and popped it into the machine. Searching through the film on the monitor, I found myself glancing over at the librarian, feeling on guard, knowing the tall man was nearby. I couldn't stop myself from spacing out at the sight of her flowered dress. I talked myself into doing a few breathing exercises as I gathered my composure and located my document.

I've found breathing sometimes helps with my on-going case of anxiety, but remembering to breath out and stay focused is always hard, since most of the time my mind feels as though it functions in a fog.

Bingo! I found it! I pressed print on the machine and got up from the hard seat, feeling the stiffness in my back.

"Well I'm all finished now," I said as I walked up to the counter.

"That's great; did you find everything you were looking for?"

"Yes I did, thank you for your help," I said staring at her dress. She leaned under the counter to retrieve the paper in the printer. I scrunched my nose and thought, *there's something really strange about that dress.*

"Here you go sweetie," she said, handing me my article.

"Thank you."

I turned to head toward the exit and a tingling sensation came over me.

I walked out into the twilight evening, heading toward my car, stepping down two steps, and <u>wham!</u> I felt like I just hit a brick wall. I stopped dead in my tracks.

"Her dress! It's her dress," I said aloud. "Shit. It's the friggin' dress."

Her dress looks just like the librarian's dining room wallpaper! I walked slowly down the remaining six steps and across the wide sidewalk. I began to feel this powerful twisting and turning in my stomach as an anxiety attack took hold. *Dammit, where are my Pepto-Bismol tablets when I need them?* Feelings of utter sadness came over me as I opened my car door and sat in the driver's seat. I thought about the red and pink flowered wallpaper pasted in the house of the librarian who lived up the street from us when I was a child. Closing the car door slowly; suddenly I felt cold and began to tremble. I took a few deep breaths, started the car, and hit the dial on the heater, turning it up high. *The librarian who lived up the street wore her hair in a bun, too;* flashes from the past entered my head.

I turned up the blower and placed my face right in front of the dashboard vent. *Oh my God! The spilled milk, the snow, the cold freezing snow.* My head began to spin, feeling the blood rush to my face. Putting my hands on my cold cheeks, wiping away the sweat, I remember *my poor feet; they are so cold, the snow, how I hate the snow.* Then the flashback began playing full force, taking hold of me like I was an orange being squeezed to make juice. Leaning my head on the steering wheel as my mind relived the past, I felt myself quiver as I rocked back and forth to comfort myself while the mini-movie played.

The Memory

It's the middle of the night, and the year is 1972. I'm seven years old and wake to the sounds of my thirteen year old sister, Barbra, screaming, crying profusely, pleading with pure fear in her voice.
"Please, please. No! No!"
Getting out of bed I check my feet to make sure my socks are on. Quietly I walk down the curved staircase. I can still hear her screaming, pleading with someone, but can't hear the other person. I know who it is, though. Reaching the bottom of the staircase undetected, I peek around the corner into the living room.
Oh no! Dad's here.
There's Barbra at the front door bent over like she's got a tummy ache and crying. She won't stop crying, I feel scared; very scared, terrified. *Please God, don't let him get into the house, please, please,* I pray.
I know what's going to happen next; it happens all the time. Very bad things. He's drunk again and full of rage; he's mad someone locked the front door before going to bed, and now we will all pay. Even though I'm only seven, I know what I need to do before it all starts. I look down at my feet again to make sure I still have my socks on. I debate with myself whether or not I should take the socks off; if I take them off, I can run faster, but if I leave them on that'll be safer. I hear him scream through the door just as I flinch with fear.
I dash back up the stairs to wake my five-year-old sister Marcia, who's sleeping on the top bunk of our bed.
"Marcia, get up! Get up! We have to go! We have to run! Barbra is going to open the door. Hurry! Hurry!" I yell, "Dad is here."
Marcia jumps off the bunk bed. She knows there's no time to put shoes on; we have to move very quickly. *It's so hard running in nightgowns,* I think, fleetingly. Marcia and I know what to do when the bad things happen. There's no need ex-

plaining; she checks her own feet for socks. We both know if we don't wear our socks, our feet will get cut; because the ice has crusted over the top of the snow. It's bad enough to run out into the frigid air without a coat, hat, gloves or a scarf, but to run onto the crusted snow barefoot is painful and dangerous. The cuts bleed, and it takes a really long time to warm our feet once we get back home. We have all learned that our feet are more important to our safety than those other items of clothing.

I tell Marcia to wait for me at the bottom of the stairs because I need to wake up Mom. Marcia's very smart. She knows to wait, but she also knows that if Dad gets in the house, she must run. I quickly run down the hall into my parents' bedroom. The door's wide open. I enter the threshold, and before I can say a word I see my mother lying on her bed with her eyes wide open, wearing her robin's-egg blue robe. She hears the screams. She knows. *Why is she just lying there?* Just then I get a jolt of reality when I hear the door bounce open and hit the wall. I gasp with fright. Loud footsteps and screaming ring through the lower level of the house.

"Get the fuck over here you cock sucking mother fucking cunt; you are going to wish you were never fucking born you fucking cunt-faced bitch," my father screams.

I have no time to say anything to my mother. Startled by the loud noises, I jump and take off running out of her bedroom, down the hall, swinging around the newel post. My head begins to feel fuzzy. My keen sense of danger kicks in—my stomach begins to tighten and a tingling sensation attacks my neck.

My socks give way as my nightgown acts like a sled and I slide down the stairs. My face feels hot and I cover my mouth with both my hands so I won't scream. I slide down to the bottom step where I find Marcia scrunched up into a ball with her knees up to her chin and her head pinned against her knees. She's scared out of her mind, rocking back and forth and shaking. I grab her arm and we head through the living room and toward the front door. I hear Barbra scream for her life as she runs toward the kitchen door in the back of the house.

"Help! God he is going to kill me! Help please! *Help, Help, Help!*" She screams, with a high-pitched curdle to her voice.

Mom comes running down the stairs, yelling hysterically, "Get out! Get out!" while waving her arms and motioning us toward the front door.

"I'm going to get you, you little fucking bitch!" he yells, chasing Barbra out the kitchen door and into the back yard.

Running toward the entry, I glance over into the dining room, which is between the living room and kitchen. I feel like throwing up as the image of the dining room shocks my sight. The heavy antique table has been turned over on its side, and the chairs are scattered throughout the room, upside down.

I make it out the front door and into the frigid air with my mother and sister. We run very fast up the steep hill, with Marcia trailing behind. We run up to our school librarian's house where we'll be safe. The librarian has a big deck off the back of her house that we often hide under until my father passes out or leaves and comes back in the morning. That always takes time—an hour or longer—so we squat under the deck in the cold and wait. We just wait.

"I hope he doesn't come looking for us," I whisper to Marcia. "I hate it when he finds us."

Marcia looks up at me with her arms tightly wrapped around her legs; her teeth are chattering, she nods in agreement.

"I hope the librarian doesn't hear us out here," Mom whispers.

"Her kitchen light is on. Do you think she heard us?" Marcia asks. I can tell from her voice that she's panicking.

"I hope Barbra got away," I said. I'm dreading what could have happened. "She was really screaming loud as she ran through the back yard."

"She can run pretty fast," Mom says. She sounds confident, but I just hope Barbra doesn't trip and fall. If she does, Dad will for sure get her and bash her head into the ground.

"I'm just going to take a peek around the house," I say as I crawl out from under the deck. I lightly touch the cold siding of the house, creeping my head around the corner to watch for his car.

"Where are you going?" my mother demands. "Sit back down. He might be driving around looking for us."

"How ugly."

"What?" Marcia asks. Her breathing is labored still from our dash up the hill.

"The librarian's wallpaper," I say, "It's ugly."

"Sit down, please Holly" Marcia begs. "I don't want him to find us." Marcia's shivering, and her voice trembles as she whispers.

"That's right Holly, you know what will happen if he finds us. He'll beat you girls with his belt and smack you hard in the head and face. He'll grab you by your hair and throw us in the car and take us home and scream and yell at me until he passes out," Mom whispers with blue smoke coming from the corners of her mouth, "and right now your father is beating up the house." Mom says placing her hands over her face.

Dad's known to destroy the house when we're not inside. He drives around in hopes of locating us. I don't know why or what we've done but if he catches us he'll beat us. Not my mother, though. I've never seen him hit my mother. He calls her bad names too, and I don't know why but if he catches us, he'll call her a stupid kite. Tonight though, he hunts for us, his children, all girls. We're bitches and sluts, weak and worthless. That's what he always says.

"It's been about an hour now. Should we walk back down and see if he's still in there?" Mom asks as the cold smoke surrounds her mouth.

"I'm freezing. I want to go to bed," Marcia says. Her teeth are chattering and I notice her lips turning blue. "The cold, snowy rocks under this deck are hurting my feet."

"Ok, but let's go in between the houses, in case he's still driving around," I tell them while blowing my breath into my freezing hands. "I'm scared he'll find us and catch us."

"Me too," Marcia says. "I don't like it when he catches us."

We return to our trashed house. We are all cold and shivering. My father has left, and the house looks as though it was hit by a tornado. Glass is all over the living room floor, and as I walk into the kitchen, I have to tiptoe over the food that was once tucked away in the refrigerator. The walls have ketchup splattered on them and as I look up toward the ceiling, I notice a salad dressing bottle sticking out of the wall. For some odd reason, I really feel sorry for that bottle of salad dressing.

Moving over to the refrigerator, I notice the mint green and white speckled linoleum floor is no more—it's all white from the milk that's been thrown. The milk is everywhere—the walls, the puke-green-colored stove, the sea-foam-green cabinet doors—it's even splattered on the kitchen window over the sink. I feel so ashamed and sad, standing with my hands together and shivering from the cold. My flannel nightgown with pink flowers and ruffles around the collar isn't keeping me very warm.

My eyes began filling up with tears and I take long deep breaths to try and relieve myself of the pain in my heart and stomach. *I wish I could disappear. Why does this always happen?* I don't know where my sisters are, I can't hear them. My body feels numb and my head feels fuzzy again. That always happens to me after the bad things happen, my head feels fat and I can't hear any sounds.

I squat down, poking my finger in the spilled milk on the floor, swirling the milk in circles. Warm tears fall onto my rosy cold cheeks and the bottom ruffle of my flannel nightgown falls into the milk puddle.

"Go to bed Holly," Mom says as she begins cleaning the mess in the kitchen. "Everything will be better tomorrow."

Tired and lonely, I slug my way up the stairs and into my room. I know when I get upstairs my room will be a mess just like the rest of the house. My mattress will be off its frame and I'll find my blanket and pillow somewhere on the floor. I know I'll get into trouble at school tomorrow for falling asleep in class again.

Slowly I walk into my room with my head held down. I shut the light. Grabbing my things that were thrown across my room, I slowly flop onto my bed with my blanket and pillow. I hear Marcia squirming on the top bunk. Looking over at the moonlit window I hear Barbra coming up the stairs sobbing.

"Try to get some sleep," I say softly. "Tomorrow will be better."

And it is. The next morning, the house is clean and shows no signs that the tornado-like rage of my father had hit it. There is never any evidence of the nightmares. My mother stays up all night cleaning, until the cycle happens all over again.

A Healing Story...

"Mourning Mommy" 2005

 The garage is filled with the sounds of Johann Pachelbel's "Canon in D." The music bounces off the walls. I dip my hands in the dark blue acrylic paint and begin my healing by taking in the music of the strings as I smash my hands on the four-foot by four-foot canvas I have spread out on the floor of the garage. I swirl my hands over the canvas in circles as I feel like dancing in the clouds of the classical tones. I begin to feel the little girl inside of me well up with tears of sadness and pain. I take in deep breaths; the sounds of the violins and cello are air filling my lungs.

 My spirit starts to descend into the deep realms of my past as the small child in me remembers the cold nights under the librarian's deck. My tears fall onto the crusted, ice covered snow. I imagine my little body squatting, shivering from the terror of being alive with no one to protect me from the horrors that lurk in the night, hunting for me. Bursting out the cries for this little girl inside, my hands swirled through the different shades of blue.

Just then my husband, Steve, walks in as my mind and soul are immersed in the macabre past.

"Holly, what's this painting of?" He grabs a lawn chair and takes a seat. I don't answer; I only hear the relaxing, strong sounds of Pachelbel's masterpiece. I look deep into the past while sliding my hands across the white canvas. Although I sense his presence, I'm not ready to leave my spirit of healing to start up a conversation.

I move slowly with the music as I push my hands with my body, gliding through the paint, making my work of art. I take in the composition, knowing Steve is viewing my every movement as I make new strokes.

I take in another deep breath, sit back on my bare heels and look toward him, holding up my blue colored hands.

"I love this part of healing," I say cracking a smile. "It brings out so much energy." I feel completely exhausted.

"What's this one about?" he asks as the harmony of the music changes from strings to flutes.

"Remember the stories I told you about running into the night, into the cold? About the ice, my poor feet, and the hiding under the librarian's deck?" I ask.

"Yes, I remember." He looks confused, bringing his hand to his chin, a nervous habit of his. He glances at the canvas on the concrete floor.

"This painting will be titled 'Mourning Mommy.' I'm depicting the mommy I mourn, the one who didn't protect me," I say, not hiding the desolation I feel. The music shifts from flutes to the harp.

"That's powerful." He blinks with understanding.

"Good. It touches you," I say while dipping my hands in the whites—ivory and cream.

"What do the colors of white represent?" he asks as he shifts himself in the green-striped lawn chair.

"The whites represent my soul and the blues represent my cries," I answer, wiping a bead of sweat off my forehead with my wrist, then swiping a tear from my cheek.

The tune switches again from the harp to the piano as I skim across the canvas, synchronized with the music. Steve watches without interrupting as I finish my masterpiece of grieving.

Squatting, I roll back on my heels and plop my butt on the cold concrete floor. Bending my head, holding the sides of my cheeks with the palms of my paint stained hands, I lean my elbows on my knees. I let out a slight whimper.

"Are you okay?" Steve asks.

I shake my head in response and swallow as I feel sorrow for this scared little girl in my chest.

I lift my head.

"You know, living through the abuse is painful..."

"Living with the effects is painful..."

I swallow again.

"And working through the healing process is painful..."

"All of this work I do on healing feels as though I am throwing out internal garbage. Emotional garbage, is what I call it, that is what all this STUFF is..."

"I feel as though I'm purging this emotional garbage, and it sucks," I say, wiping a warm tear across my cheek.

"It's worth it, ya know? All this healing, all this hard work, it's worth it. I feel as though I'm making room inside my head and body for the things I want to put there. Even though it's scary as hell and hurts deep inside, it's incredibly liberating."

My emotions in painting this piece land me with feelings of melancholy. It's common for me to take in my feelings, sit with them, honoring them, until they detach and flow out of my body. I never know how long this will take, but at some point the grieving will lift, healing my essence within.

Pachelbel and I finish harmoniously. I pull the canvas up from the floor and stand it up against the concrete wall to dry. I look over at Steve, who is sitting in the lawn chair with his legs crossed, his hand still holding his chin as he stares at the painting.

"What do you think?" I ask, wiping my hands with a paper towel.

"Wow!" He says, standing from the chair, "I don't know what to say. It's amazing the way you bring the colors together and move them around as if you already have the picture in your head." He puts the chair away on its hook and turns to me.

"I need to wash my hands now," I say, staring at the painting.

Steve walks toward me and gives me a kiss on my forehead.

"The hard work in healing is finally working," he says, grabbing for the doorknob as he walks toward the house. I shut off the garage lights behind him and then look back at my painting and whisper, "You're safe now." I walk back into the house and close the door behind me.

*　　　*　　　*

As my healing process begins to evolve, I've found many forms of therapy, one of which is art. Healing through art has had a tremendous impact of my journey. I often see my art therapy as an inner personal struggle being worked out through paint and canvas. My paintings tell a story of their own; they tell the story of my emotions. My artwork comes through me as I feel my way through life; I am one with the paint. I do not use objects such as brushes. I simply use my hands. For me, my hands are the paint brushes. With every stroke I make, I gain a sense of restorative wholeness.

Chapter 2
Pretty Face

The Trigger – 2001

Sitting on the back porch at my sister Marcia's house, I looked around and noticed how her yard is so perfect. Every rock looks like it's been placed into a bed of colorful flowers with care. The well-groomed pine trees seem to have dropped into her yard right out of an arboretum. The flowers are bright as sunshine, their colors luminous and rich, like a painter's pallet. The bushes have been nicely trimmed with clean edges. I couldn't help but think to myself, *what a perfect yard. Too perfect.*

I haven't spoken to my sister in a few years, but we've decided to get together during my visit back to my Nebraska hometown. My observation of Marcia is that she seems to live such an ideal life. Everything in her home has its place, and her car is just as immaculate.

Marcia has managed to make everything around her appear just right, so clean, but we know better. We know things are never as wonderful as they appear. After all, she grew up in the same home I grew up in. We were children of abuse and now we're adults who have been affected by that abuse; nothing will change that.

Marcia walked out onto the back porch where I was sitting soaking up the sun. Our relationship is strained, and we're clearly two very different people. We sit, she and I, two sisters of a time when our lives were not normal. We shared our "holocaust" not in words, but in the tender togetherness of simply knowing; understanding with a look, a nod, a touch of the hand. Even without words, we still hold a connection to each other. Sitting there across from me, I could see the apprehension in her eyes; she turned to look away from me. *I'm sure my presence only reminded her of the past that can't fit into the flawless world she has created for herself.* The truth of our backgrounds are not something either one of us wants to remember.

"Move on, forgive and forget, stop living in the past," is what I've always been told. *Silly little phrases*, I think, *these phrases hold no value to a survivor. No one else has the right to be the deciding factor of when another heals his or her pain.* I looked around at the cleanliness and thought, *maybe this is her way of sweeping away the past.*

Marcia and I sat, drinking our tea and soaking the beautiful day into our memories like two south sea turtles washed ashore on a pristine Tahitian beach. We sat together for a while, looking out at the lovely yard. I stared at the back garden and told her how picturesque it looked.

"Yes, it does look good," she replied. I then realized that Marcia *is* her flowers. She grew them tenderly with a caring touch. I envy her ability to mind her garden, a skill I do not possess.

I asked if she's seen our parents, a subject that is no doubt one Marcia would prefer not to discuss. I could sense her tension in her breath. I felt her body tighten as I tightened mine. I felt her anxiety as the image of our parents entered her mind. She squinted her eyes and cocked her head.

"I've seen Dad speeding through town, but haven't seen Mom," she responded, reluctantly.

I know she hasn't spoken to our parents in some years. And, I know the subject hurts her and makes her sad, just as it does me. It showed in her heavy breathing and droopy eyes, as she placed her hand on her chest.

Although this visit is a strained one, Marcia and I were able to chat together in a relaxed manner, and the more we talked, the more our conversation drifted to our childhood and the abuse we both endured.

I felt a bit anxious myself; I had a question to ask Marcia. I was scared and felt as though my body was shaking inside at what her reaction would be. I took a deep breath, as I found myself explaining to Marcia that I want to write a book about the abuse. I wanted to know how she would feel, and I wanted to know if reading my book would be upsetting to her. I had so many conflicting feelings writing a book about my child abuse; I felt as though I cared more about everyone else's feelings than my own.

Marcia gave me a look that almost appeared to be fear. Her hazel eyes widened and a pale appearance flushed over her warm, tanned face. Then she looked off and smiled upon her children, who were playing catch in the yard. *I wonder if she catches herself in moments of melancholy, thinking to herself that her children are the age she was when she suffered childhood terror.*

"Sure, you can write a book, sounds like a good idea," she said turning to look at me with a crooked smile and a raised eyebrow.

Is she patronizing me? I could sense tension in her strained voice, and I knew this could ruin the perfect world she had made for herself. *Maybe I'm being selfish?*

I knew if I put everyone else's feelings before my own, I would not be satisfied with my decision. *What am I to do?* Writing the book might only add to our already damaged relationship, or it might bring us closer. *Should I risk it? Would she ever come to understand that this is important to me, to my healing?* Then it dawned on me, the conflicting thoughts. *Am I asking my sister for permission? Of course,* questioning myself, it all has to do with the unwritten rule of protecting the secret. I had always perceived the "family secret" to be something that needed preserving, as if the secret itself deserved to be shielded, and now by writing a book, I'm blowing the whistle.

Gathering my thoughts, I got ready to leave, feeling as if I've just opened Pandora's Box and my sister wants no part of it. Opening the front door to walk out, I turned to face her, wanting to express my enjoyment in our visit. We embraced each other and as I pulled away, I noticed the look on her face was like that of a hurt child. Her mouth was pouting and her eyes were fatigued. Staring at her face took me back in time to when I saw Marcia's pretty face, her sweet face as a young child. Suddenly, upon giving her a kiss on the cheek I felt hurt and sad looking into my little sister's face. I could see the horror--the pain--of how her spirit had been broken.

Driving away I remembered my younger sister's small round face, and knew she could control her depression within the confines of a compulsion to clean, to adjust, to paint, to preserve a beauty that was destroyed in her youth.

I need to write my book, not just for myself, but for Marcia and for Barbra, too. I wish for Marcia to see the warmth in her flowers. I want my sisters to fly like butterflies, free from the gravity of earth, fluttering in the sunshine. I wish for them to live life, not just survive it by living in a trance caused by their past.

*   *   *

The Memory....

Today is a great day. Summer is near and I can't wait until school lets out for summer break. The end of third grade is creeping up on me, but for now I'm still eight years old and the year is 1974. I'm happy today because no bad things happened last night, no bad things happened this morning, and I didn't fall asleep in class.

The bell rings, and I grab my books and head outside to meet Marcia. Today we're going to make a fort for our Barbie dolls and I'm so excited. I run down the long hall of our old school building to greet Marcia at the first grade door.

"Good afternoon, Holly," Mrs. Banister says.

"Good afternoon, Mrs. Banister."

I glance in Mrs. Banister's room looking for Marcia, but don't see her. *Maybe she went outside to wait.*

"I sure hope she didn't leave without me," I say out loud as I spin around in circles looking at the empty halls. Walking down a few steps, I take a flying leap to the landing by jumping three steps, pushing open the big oak glass door to the outside. I take in the smells of the fresh air, of summer coming.

I look all over the playground for Marcia, but she isn't here. I walk all around the big brick school building yelling for her, but she is nowhere to be found. *She's supposed to wait for me, if I don't find her, I'll get into trouble.* I look around the dark brick school building one last time, then across the street toward the rickety bridge I hate to cross. Turning around, I look across toward the playground where the rusted out swing set sits. She isn't anywhere in sight. I begin to panic, and immediately close my hands into fists and pray I find her while walking home. *I hate walking over the big bridge by myself, I just hate it.*

"Oh why aren't you here Marcia? I hate this bridge," my voice quivers.

I'm terrified of heights, and petrified of this rickety concrete bridge. The two horizontal guard rail poles are very low, and the bridge goes over the interstate below, cars passing underneath at top speed.

I'm brave, I can cross this nasty bridge if I stay very close to the inside part of the bridge near the road, the part that doesn't look onto the interstate below.

During the rest of my walk home I think of reasons to give my parents as to why I didn't walk home with Marcia.

She ran off without me, I thought, coming up with something to say. *She wasn't near the playground so I left; I looked everywhere and couldn't find her.*

I think and worry all the way home, but when I get to the front door I have no excuse. *What do I say? Think. Think.* But nothing comes to my head. *I know what I'll do, I'll just burst the door open, very happily and cheerily, and announce to the house I'm home.*

"I'm home house!" I yell with feigned excitement, "I'm home, Mom."

Marcia's curled up on couch in the living room, sitting with her face in the red and black Mexican patterned pillows.

"Marcia where were you?" I ask angrily.

"I looked all over for you, and how did you get home so fast?"

Marcia turns and looks at me. When I see her, I gasp.

"Oh my God!"

Just then, I remembered Marcia never went to school today cuz she was sick or somthin. I've seen a lot of bad things, but Marcia's face is something new. Her face is covered with bruises—small bruises all over her perfectly-framed round face. Her tan complexion is now blue and purple. There are bruises all over her forehead and cheeks; her pert nose and eyelids are covered with these small little purple marks. Her skin is swollen, and even her usually pale rose lips are blue.

"What happened to you?" I ask. "Tell me, who did this? How did this happen?" I press.

"Mom," she says in a whisper as she buries her face back into the pillow.

In shock and gasping, I ask, "How? When? Why?"

"Your sister fell out of the tree," Mom says entering the spotless living room, tossing a dishrag over her shoulder.

I might only be a kid, but I'm not stupid. I know a tree fall can't do that; I've fallen out of trees before, but I know better than to question my mother, as my brown eyes follow her movement around the room. I feel a lump in my throat and a fluster of warmth to my face as I look up at her in fear.

"If anyone at school asks you what happened to your sister, you tell them she fell out of a tree," Mom says pointing her long fingernail at me while taking a seat in her red velvet chair.

With sadness filling up inside and tears forming in my eyes, I look down at Marcia and say nothing, and remain silent the rest of the day.

During the night, no other bad things happen, no throwing of household items, no beatings and most importantly, no running out of the house in the middle of the night. I'm sick of running out of the house. I've been doing that ever since I was a baby wearing pajamas with feet. The only thing happening tonight is Dad's yelling at Mom for Marcia's face.

All snuggled up in our matching nightgowns and bedspreads, and with our bunk beds now separated, I lay looking at Marcia's purple face.

"How did it happen?"

"She got mad cuz I went out on my bike after my bath," she says stroking her face with her small hand.

"Did she punch you in the face?"

"No, the stove punched me in the face."

"Huh, the stove punched you, how did that happen?"

"She slammed my face in the stove, a bunch of times; I don't remember, it was a lot."

"Does it hurt?"

"Real bad," tears run onto her pillow. "Does it look real bad?"

"It's poofy, and it smells."

"Huh? It smells, like what?"

"Like…I dunno, you know… how bruises normally smell."

"Will it go away?" She whispers with a pout on her mouth. "What about tomorrow at school? What will I do? The kids will laugh."

"The bruises always go away," I tell her. "Remember when Dad pinned Barbra to the floor and slapped her real hard on the sides of her face?"

Marcia nods with remembrance.

"That went away and the bruise on my side from when he hit me with the horse whip a bunch of times went away, and besides Barbra always has yellow and blue marks, and those always go light. Yours'll go away too," sucking on a tuft of hair.

"I don't know what we will do about the kids at school," Marcia quivers.

"Try to get some sleep. Everything will be better tomorrow." I covered my head with my pink blanket.

The stress on Mom is trickling down hill now. I figure out the only way not to get caught in her wrath is to try really hard to be on her good side. If I listen to her and do what she asks, I won't have to worry about getting beaten by her. For the most part it works; Marcia's not so lucky, though.

The next morning, the house remains quiet. Barbra leaves soon after she wakes. She hates Mom and Dad. I feel sorry for her because she's always getting beaten and called names. The only one she likes is Bop, Mom's dad. He had to take her away one summer because Dad beat on her too much, but she had to come back for school.

Walking down the winding stairs with Marcia, we see Mom standing at the bottom of the stairs wearing her neatly pressed multi-colored muumuu.

"I need to talk to you," she looks at me with her black piercing eyes.

Marcia heads into the kitchen while mom wraps her delicate hand with long fingernails around my arm and drags me into the living room. She reminds me of the small lie I have to tell people if anyone asks about Marcia's bruised face.

"Remember, if anyone asks you about Marcia's face, you tell them she fell out of a tree, do you understand?" she says with an impatient whisper.

I respond with a nod for fear of waking my father.

"Good now, go eat your Malt-O-Meal and get off to school. You have fifteen minutes." I run toward the kitchen.

Mom doesn't drive, and even if she did, there certainly wouldn't be a ride awaiting us. Besides, Mom needs all her energy for when Dad wakes up.

Out the door, Marcia and I start off on our two-mile walk to school. I want to ask her about the school and what Mom told me to say, but I'm too scared. She's walking with her head down and her shimmering straight dark brown hair is covering her face. Marcia starts to look like me; I always wear my hair in my face, always.

"If you push your hair more towards the sides of your face and hold your head down all day, maybe no one will notice."

"Yeah, I know." She brushes her hair toward her face with her pudgy little hands.

"Your hair is easier to put in your face, it's curly, mine won't stay."

"We're getting close to school now, just do your best and I'll figure out what to say."

We approach the school grounds. The kids are gathered on the playground. Walking up to the black top I begin to fear the kids making fun of my sister's face, and then making fun of me. They come up to us one by one asking what happened, but neither my sister nor I say a word. I'm afraid and I know Marcia feels the same. *Everyone's going to know about our home, the things that happen there and they'll make fun of us.* Marcia grabs my arm. I can tell from her grip that she's terrified.

"Don't tell them the truth, Holly. Tell them the lie, tell them I fell out of the tree, please Holly, please. I don't want to get into more trouble, please," Marcia begs.

A pudgy blonde girl walks up to us while bouncing a pink ball.

"What happened to your face, Marcia?" We walk closer to the school playground.

"Yeah, Marcia what happened?" Another girl asks while smacking gum in her mouth, when more kids circle us.

"Oh, my God!! Marcia your face looks awful," a red-headed freckled-faced girl says gasping for air while slapping her hands on her cheeks.

I remember the lie I'm supposed to tell, but nothing comes out. I want to spit out the lie, so everyone will leave us alone. Marcia lets go of my arm and runs over by the steps of the big oak double doors to the school and sits down on one of the concrete steps.

"What happened to your sister?"

Standing there with all these kids asking questions about my sister's face, I feel my hands clench into fists. I feel like screaming at all the questions. I hate attention. I don't want anyone to know about the bad things that happen in our house. I feel so ashamed. I feel like hiding, and I know Marcia feels like hiding too, looking over at her covering her face in her lap. We're good at hiding, but neither of us can hide from this.

"Leave her alone," I yell. "Stop asking all these questions! Stop it, just stop!" I begin to shake.

A fat, pointed-nosed teacher comes up, takes me aside by my arm and walks me away from the crowd. I look over at Marcia again and see her widened eyes and raised eyebrows, the look of fright.

"What happened to your sister's face?" the teacher demands as she shakes my arm. Looking up at her, I think, *Why do you care, you bitch? I hate this school and you teachers. You are all mean and nasty.* One teacher liked to slap us with a ruler on our hands and another teacher always takes students into the coat closet to spank us on our butts with a hard wooden board she calls her "board of education." I know cuz I got spanked once in that closet and had to hike my dress up so she could see my bottom. I don't trust these people. I hate them and I know if I tell the little lie I'm supposed to tell, they will know it and I'll get slapped for lying. But I don't want to tell the truth either, because I don't trust them; the whole school will find out and make fun of us.

"Well, what happened to your sister? Are you going to answer me? Do I need to call your mother?" The teacher asks, spit spraying in my face.

Standing there looking up at her pointed nose, feeling so afraid and so confused, out of nowhere the words fly from my mouth.

"My mother beat her," I spit out quickly.

I can't believe it. I said it. I didn't lie. I was sure I'd be a coward and say something stupid and get myself in trouble, but I didn't. I told the truth. I'm very concerned for me and Marcia, but I don't care. I told the truth. I push the teacher's iron grip off my arm and run and sit with Marcia until the bell rings.

*   *   *

Nothing ever happened to me for telling the truth and I doubt the school called my mother. Nothing was ever done; the school did nothing; the teacher did nothing. This, after all, was a family problem. That wouldn't be the last time Marcia would have a bruised face, and we all knew what it was like to have bruises. Yet no one ever did anything to help, so telling the school was a waste of time. They didn't care. I realized later that maybe the reason no one ever did anything was because, behind the covered up bruises and marks, we were kept very clean and well-groomed.

*   *   *

A Healing Story....

For my sister Marcia...

I found a picture of you and me sitting on chairs in our old home. I was maybe eight or nine and you were maybe seven.

Even though we are only 20 months apart in age, I am older and wished somehow I could have protected you.

It was such a strange feeling seeing this old, dark picture. The paper has lost its glossy texture and the edges are dried and torn. The wallpaper on the kitchen wall is in the photo along with the green chair rail that looks at least five feet from the floor. As many times as I have written about the bad things that happened in that home, I forgot about that God-awful looking green fruit wallpaper, seeing it again reminds me of how real it all was. The chairs were hideous as well; they were a puke green floral. Do you remember? With black steel legs that were no doubt very fashionable back in the early 70s. I look at myself in this picture with a great sense of shame and sadness. *Poor sad children.* I'm sitting like a little statue with my back extended and my small hands folded together. My face has this rather fake, yet forced smile. And you, Marcia, are slumped over like a sloth, sitting on one of those puke green chairs. We are both wearing the same outfits; yours blue and mine red. Little two-piece outfits that show our midriffs, with ruffled edges on the top and bottom. Although I don't remember these outfits, I think, *don't they look cute?*

Your smile looks as though you were told to say "cheese" and like the good girl you always were, you showed all of her teeth. As for me, no teeth show, just a stiff-lipped smile, to go along with my stony appearance.

I feel great sorrow for these two little girls. They lived such a horrific life with those people who identified themselves as their parents. Then, out of nowhere I begin to laugh. The feelings of sadness have now been overshadowed with happy, joyful feelings at seeing these two children.

It's my sister and I. We are together, and how I miss you, my sister. I think I will go visit you the next chance I get. Then I laugh at that god-awful wallpaper and those puke green chairs. I remember the feeling of those vinyl chairs and how they scratched my legs because they were so ripped, torn and tattered.

I never have in my life put up pictures in my home of my family. It just was something that wasn't very important to me, and I didn't care to see them. Maybe I should. I think now I would like to see these beautiful girls; they deserved to have their pictures displayed. I will put up this picture of you and me. I have a cute little frame I brought back with me from one of my trips to Israel, and now this picture of my sister and me has a home.

This picture now sits in my kitchen, so every day when I do dishes, or simply walk past, I look at us and I'm reminded of how lucky I am to have had you for a sister while growing up. I think about how we played Barbies together and how we would fight with the boys in the neighborhood. But most of all I think about how you would be there with me when we needed to hide. I wasn't alone; I had you, my beautiful little sister, with the pretty face.

Chapter 3

The Skipper Doll

The Trigger -- 1990

Walking through the halls of the Golden-Crest assisted living facility, I searched for room 246. Mrs. Kaplan is waiting for me to give her a manicure.
"Mrs. Kaplan, I'm here to give you a manicure," I call as I enter her room. I looked around and saw no Mrs. Kaplan. I pulled out my scratched up note pad from my torn brown bag to check the room number and name. *Yep, room 246, Mrs. Kaplan, small woman with attitude*, I have scribbled.
I placed my bag containing my manicure equipment down on the newly made forest-green blanketed bed. I walked over to the freshly cleaned bathroom that smelled of bleach.
"Mrs. Kaplan, are you in here?" I called again slowly opening the metal door, feeling panic and a churn of my stomach.
No answer. I walked out into the hall only to find a four-tiered metal cart full of empty lunch trays. I began to feel sweat beads form on my forehead as thoughts of not finding this client spun through my mind. My hypersensitive responses began to activate as my mind conjured up thoughts of

self-blame for not finding this woman. I reached in my worn purse and pulled out a Pepto-Bismol tablet and threw it in my mouth to chew, hoping, to calm my nerves.

Oh, great! If this woman has an attitude, she will for sure be upset with me for being late for her appointment. God how I hate this job! I turned around to head back into Mrs. Kaplan's room, just when a woman from behind me yelled in a booming, gregarious voice, "Are you looking for Mrs. Kaplan?"

I nearly jumped out of my skin, turning around and seeing an older, 80-ish looking woman wearing a neon pink robe.

"Yes, do you know where she is?"

"Ya, she's down the hall in the play room. And sorry for startling you, I can see you scare easy. I can't hear that well, so I shout," she said, her dentures slipping on to her tongue.

"Okay thank you, I'll find her." I noticed one of my hands clinching into a fist. I shook it off and grabbed my bag from the bed.

Taking in a deep breath I headed out into the hall and thought, *wow, by the look of the curlers in that lady's hair, I bet she once knew how to roll a mean curl. And that make-up on her face, Oy vey. It looks like the work of a three-year-old. Poor thing.*

"I hope my kids never put me in a place like this," I mumbled.

Quickly moving down the hall, I found myself in front of the playroom. Walking into the bright, light, colorful room I noticed one of my dirty worn tennis shoes was untied. I bent down to tie my soiled shoe-lace, when I sensed someone standing over me. Hairs on the back of my neck stood up as I looked up and noticed it was an orderly dressed in white.

"Sir," I whispered with a hard swallow, "I'm here to see Mrs. Kaplan."

The huge man with a goatee beard and bald head said in a squeaky voice, "She's over there dressing her dolls."

"Ok, thank you." I looked and noticed her sitting at a sky-blue round table.

Briskly walking over, I grasped my brown bag with a sweaty tight grip. *I hope she isn't angry at my tardiness.*
"Mrs. Kaplan." I reached over, placing my hand gently on her shoulder. "I'm here to give you a manicure, your son Paul has sent me," I said smiling as I plopped my bags on the table.

The blonde-haired, fragile looking woman responded, "Ahh hehh! You are here to manicure these old tried hands and make them look pretty?"

"Yes, yes I am, ma'am."

She seems peaceful enough, I deemed with a sense of relief. *I'll just manicure her right here in the playroom.*

Filing Mrs. Kaplan's brittle nails, she proceeded to tell me all about her doll collection.

"This is my doll, Carrie," she says, "and this is my doll, Georgia, aren't they pretty?"

"Yes, very pretty, where did you get them?"

"I got them......hummmm.....I got them."

"Yes."

"I'm thinking," she declared, "I can't remember, you young girls always ask hard questions."

"Ok, we don't have to talk about the dolls anymore."

Ending the doll conversation she went on to talk about her children, two daughters and a son.

"You know I have three kids?"

"That's nice," I responded. I felt myself dissociating from reality while filing her nails.

I had no clue what Mrs. Kaplan was saying to me at that point, because I drifted off into a fog-like state. I have another disorder called, DDNOS, short for Dissociate Disorder Not Otherwise Specified. Dissociation is where I feel like my brain is going away, zoning out, feeling fuzzy. Dissociating was something I used to do as a child to make myself feel safe. As an adult, however, dissociating causes difficulty in staying completely in the present.

When I'm working I find myself disconnecting from reality because my mind feels at ease. When I'm summoned back into reality by my customer I don't have to come completely out of my dazed zone, I can easily use the term "That's nice," because it's safe and I hope no one will figure out my brain has just traveled off into in la-la land.

Mrs. Kaplan continued to talk as I continued the manicure and every now and then, I entered a state between dissociation and consciousness so I could gesture her with a nod or a simple, "uh huh." I do this so she'll think I'm paying attention to her stories, when in fact I would rather spend all day disconnecting into the safe world I've made in my head.

"Yes, and while I work," she said, "I only work part time, Harry won't have a wife that works full time; the kids go to Mrs. K's house".

"Ah huh." I focused intently on her nails as I lost concentration of her existence.

Just as I entered a state of tranquility in Holly's world, Mrs. Kaplan pulled her hands away from me and said in an uproar, "You're not paying attention to me!"

Ok, this was one of the few times I got caught at not paying attention. As much as I felt like going back into the make believe world inside my head, I knew I had to stay in the present. I felt myself drift into a state of not really being in reality. It feels as if I'm in a dream, going through the motions of life without having any feelings. All sound becomes muffled and my brain feels numb. Everything seems to be fake.

Finishing Mrs. Kaplan's manicure, I stood up from the round table as if I was a robot going through the actions of a normal day. I began to put my manicuring equipment back in my bag.

"Would you like to see my favorite doll?"

"Sure, why not." I say, not giving much thought or expression to my words.

Mrs. Kaplan hollered over to the orderly, "HEY, BOB, GET MY WHEELCHAIR!"

Bob rolled a wheel chair over and helped Mrs. Kaplan as she got into the seat.

"Come with me," she said, quickly wheeling her chair out the door. *Oy, she's going to wreck her nails.*

I grabbed the handles of the wheel chair the rest of the way down the hall toward her bedroom. Passing the tall empty food carts, I tripped over my shoelace.

"Damnit, I just tied that shoe." I feel myself coming back into reality.

"What happened?"

"Oh, nothing, I just got the lace of my tennis shoe caught in your wheel chair."

Rolling into Mrs. Kaplan's bedroom, she took charge of her wheel chair.

"There," she says while pointing toward her Howard Johnson looking nightstand. "Open the second drawer."

Reaching in, I held up a blonde-haired doll.

"She's a pretty doll," I said with a smile.

"She's my favorite."

"Awww, I remember these dolls, my sister and I used to play with Barbie and Skipper and Ken all the time," I said, remembering back in time when I played with dolls.

"So you love dolls, too?"

"Oh, yes, I remember my sister had this exact same Skipper doll."

Holding the doll up, I began to pet its hair as a smile formed on the side of my mouth.

"I remember this one time when she got poor Skipper's head all dirty," I said with a chuckle. Then my face fell into a fatigued frown. *Oh God that thought feels icky, and gross.*

Dropping my bag and purse, and placing Skipper back into Mrs. Kaplan's drawer, I felt my throat tighten and eyes fill up with tears.

"Are you all right?"

"I must go, thank you, Mrs. Kaplan."

I picked up my bags in a rush, running quickly out of the room, down the hall and out the entrance door into the fresh air. Bending over with my hands on my knees I took in a few deep breaths. Shaking, I raced over to my car as my memory of the Skipper doll flashed in my head.

*   *   *

The Memory....

It's summer 1974, and I just turned nine years old; third grade has finally ended. Today, I'm playing dolls outside on the front porch. Setting up my Barbie house, camper and all. A man comes walking up the steps of our paint-chipped front porch. I look up but can't see his face, the sun's in my eyes. The only thing I can see is his snow-white hair. The older man is a friend of my father's, so I recognize him. I don't like him; he gives me the creeps.

"Hiya," I say, as he knocks on the screen door of our house. I feel him glaring at me and I turn to look away.

"Hey kid," he says while smacking his jaw as he works his chewing gum.

I can still feel his eyes glaring at me, and that makes me feel icky inside. I put my head down so he can't see my face. I turn back to look up at him as he winks his eye at me. *Ewww, that wink gives me the creeps. I hate that yucky man.* I feel scared, and I want to run off the porch, but I'm not about to leave my Barbies by themselves.

Instead, I turn back around so fast that my long curly hair whips me in my face. I gather up my newly constructed Barbie town and decide to go play under the porch of our next-door neighbor's house, where no one will find me. *That man's gross and I don't want to be anywhere near him.*

"Hey Whitey, come on in," my father says opening the screen door.

I step down the stairs with my arms full of Barbie dolls. I look back toward the front door where Whitey stands giving me another wink.

"See ya, kid," he says popping his gum.

Yucky, nasty man!

Placing my Barbies under the neighbor's porch, I walk back to my porch to gather up my Barbie's clothes and camper. Squatting down and throwing Barbie clothes and shoes into the Barbie camper, both my parents walk out of the house. First my father walks out, snapping his fingers and walking fast, then my mother, trailing slowly behind. Dad always walks in front of Mom.

He says Mom walks too slow and men are always supposed to walk in front of women; they know their place then.

"Hey, Skinny," Dad yells, calling me by my nick-name, "My friend Whitey here's going to baby-sit you and your sister. I expect you to be good for him, he's a nice man. Don't give him any trouble, or I'll beat the shit out of you when I get home, got that?" My father barks as he briskly shuffles his way off the porch toward his car that's parked on the gravel drive. With a quick gasp of air I stand up and jump off the three porch steps and run over to the car after them.

"What? Why is *he* babysitting us? Where are you going?" I ask with a terrified tone. I'm trying to be serious so my parents will understand.

"None of your damn business half pint, now be good or else," my father yells, his voice menacing with his irritation. He pushes my forehead with the palm of his hand and backs the car out into the street.

Turning around quickly, I run back up the stairs of my porch and throw the rest of my Barbie stuff in the camper. Hurrying as fast as I can, I grab my camper and everything else that will fit into my little arms and head toward the steps. Yucky white-haired man comes out on to the porch. I freeze, squinting my eyes from the sun's shining rays, and look up at him.

"Hey kid, get in here!" he demands.

I don't want to go in, but I know if I don't I'll get in trouble, and I don't want that. I drop my camper onto the porch and walk inside the house as Whitey holds the door open for me. I stay as far away from him as I can get without scratching myself on the doorjamb.

Inside the living room, I see Marcia sitting on the couch with her knees up to her chin, leaning back on the red and black Mexican style pillow watching TV. I run over and sit next to her.

"Come over here, Squirt, and sit by me," he points to the red velvet chair.

Whitey walks over to the red velvet chair and takes a seat. I crawl off the couch, stand next to Marcia, and look at him.

"Where do you want me to sit?" I ask him nervously.

Marcia, still engrossed with a television show, has not even realized I'm standing next to her.

"Come over here and sit on my lap", he says smirking.

I clench my hands at my sides, and swallow hard. I walk slowly over to the red chair and face him. Standing in front of him, I can feel the blood rushing to my face. He leans over and grabs my shoulders with a tight grip. His hands are wide and thick. I feel petrified as his dark blue eyes are penetrating. He smiles, showing his thick yellow teeth. His skin is wrinkled, dry and dull. I swallow hard again and tighten my fists as he turns me around swiftly to face the television. I hear his belt buckle open; I tense up as he tightens his grip onto one of my shoulders. *I didn't do anything to get a spankin, why's he messin with his belt.* His hand engulfs my shoulder and neck. I take a deep breath and raise my eyebrows as I look over at Marcia, who's still engrossed in the television. I throw off his fat hand and swing back around to face his wrinkled face. He looks up at me wide-eyed while his hand is in his pants.

"Whatcha doin?"

"Don't worry about it, kid," he says with a snarl and a squint to his dark eyes.

He pulls his hand out of his pants and grabs me by my arms, swinging me back around to face the television. My legs feel weak and begin to tingle. I swallow hard again as he pulls open the back of my shorts and elastic banding from my undies. He sticks his hands inside and begins to squeeze my butt cheeks with the palms of his hands and fat fingers, probing and pulling my skin. His hand moves farther down, grabbing my sensitive parts. I stiffen myself up like a statue, tighten my fists and pray. *Oh my God, what is he doing?* I'm shaking inside, and I can feel the fear making my face hot. My head is spinning, and I'm feeling dizzy, as if I'm leaving my body. I'm going to throw up. I can't move. I feel myself float away where I begin to feel safe. Just then I'm brought back into my own skin and feel his hand is there, touching me, poking a hole inside. I want to go back to the safe feeling in my head, I can't, he won't let me. I look over at Marcia who is curled up on the couch. *Why doesn't she notice me? I want her to scream for me. I can't do it.* I want to scream so bad *please leave me alone, you dirty nasty icky, smelly man! Leave me alone just leave me alone. I don't like you; I don't like you touching me inside my undies!* I pray, *oh this hurts there.* I can't utter a word; I'm frozen like ice. I feel like dying. His fingers are big and they hurt. I feel the tears in my eyes and the heat from my face. *Please God; make him go away,* I pray as I squeeze my eyes shut.

Pulling his hands out from my underpants, he gives me a shove on my back with one of his powerful hands. I lunge forward, barely catching myself from falling.

"Go back out and play with your dolls, kid," he says in his raspy voice.

I run toward the screen door in a rush to get out, pushing the door wide open.

"Hey! You're letting in the light, shut the door," Marcia yells.

I run out onto the porch, slamming the screen door behind me. Grabbing the collar of my yellow, flowered sun top, I sit on the top step of the porch.

He's a bad man, he broke my pee pee, I think, throwing my face into my lap, rocking back and forth and tugging at my long hair around my ears. My face still feels hot, and small tears run down my cheeks while I wipe the snot with my arm. My hair gets tangled up on my sticky face and I feel sick to my stomach. My throat hurts from the lumpy feeling inside. My heart is pounding, and my legs shake as I rock back and forth, holding my arms around my small body. *Ohhhh that hurts there.*

Then I remember Marcia. She's in there with him. I stand up and wipe my nose with the bottom of my shirt. I turn around and stare at the screen door, clinching my hands back into fists. I step up the wooden step on the porch and take a deep breath, preparing myself to go back inside. Suddenly, Marcia comes running out, nearly hitting me with the screen door as she throws it open forcefully. My eyes widen as I see the scared look on her face. I step away from the flying door and slam my back into one of the porch columns. She runs off the porch, onto the gravel drive, and around to the side of the house. I leap off the porch and run to catch up with her.

"What happened?" I ask, folding my hair over my ears.

She looks at me, tears streaming down her chubby cheeks. She bends down picking a blade of grass, not saying a word.

"Come with me," I grab her hand.

"No! I don't want to go back in," she squeals.

"No, we're not going back in. We need our Barbie stuff," she lets go of my hand.

"You get it," she says backing away.

"Ok, run under the neighbor's porch," I whisper. "I'll get the camper."

I race around the house, grabbing the camper and the rest of our Barbie things. I jump off the porch with my arms full of our toys and run past the side of the house, keeping an eye on the windows in case he sees where we're going. Marcia makes it to the neighbor's porch and leaves the loose lattice in the dirt, so I'll have easy access to crawl.

We both grab the broken lattice and put it back in place so no one can see us. Lying down in the dirt, we peer out of the lattice to see if he's coming. It seems like hours are passing by as we lay there in the dirt.

"Wanna set up the Barbies?"

"Think it'll be ok?" Marcia asks warily.

"Might as well, we ain't got nothing better to do than lay here in this dirt and stare out these holes."

I busy myself with emptying out the camper.

"I hate this place," Marcia says picking up her Skipper doll.

I stare at Marcia's sad face as she drags her Skipper doll's head in the dirt.

Should I tell? NO! I'll get into trouble, that's Dad's friend. He'll lie and say we're making it all up and we'll get beat.

I can't tell Mom either, she'll think we're being dirty. She always tells us we need to keep ourselves covered up. We'll just get into trouble, big trouble; I better keep my mouth shut. Mom will get mad and Dad'll beat us, and they'll take that icky man's side.

Marcia beats Skipper's head in the dirt.

I feel like crying but only small tears fall from my eyes. Then I begin to wonder if I should tell my mother. *Can I tell my father what his yucky gross friend just did? He'll get mad at me. This is my fault. I know this is my fault. I'll get blamed. I don't know why, I just know I will.*

"I wish Barbra was home."

"Me, too."

We stay under the porch until our parents get home and Whitey leaves. We gather the Barbie town and run back home, neither of us saying a word.

Later that year…

My father comes home very upset, yelling and screaming about a car accident. I can hear him clearly as he tells my mother that Whitey is dead. I am happy he died; I want him dead. Now he can't ever touch my sister or me ever again. I run upstairs to our bedroom. Marcia is playing Barbies. I bust open the door and run over to her while she sits Indian-style on the hard linoleum floor.

"Marcia, Marcia, I have good news," I say excitedly.

"Huh, what is it, what is it?"

"Whitey's dead! He's dead, dead, dead!" I'm laughing as I give her the news. "He died in a car accident, ha, ha, ha, ha!"

"Is he really? For real? Are you sure? How do you know?"

"Heard Dad tell Mom," I whisper as I dance around, singing, "The witch is dead, the witch is dead, yahhh, the witch is DEAD!"

* * *

A Healing Poem...

Taking Our Pain Away...

Sitting out on the rocks
The ocean waves come my way
I feel rage inside as I pray
Please God take the pain inside away
The little girl inside
Hurts from being betrayed
She sits here looking so sad and dear
How can we make the pain go away?
Write out the pain on paper
Tell it like you feel
Throw it out into the sea
The waves will carry it away
The ocean waves crash our way
Swallowing up our paper of pain
A young girl comes near
Looking so sad and dear
Take some paper I say
On that write and pray
Throw it into the ocean
The waves will carry the pain away
I leave you my paper
And my pen I say
As a young man comes our way
Looking so sad and dear
The ocean takes the pain away

Chapter 4

The Clothes Line

The Trigger — 2002

Sitting on an El-Al flight in final descent into the Ben-Gurion airport in Tel-Aviv, I looked over at my best friend, Pamela, who was smiling from ear to ear.
"I'm excited, are you?" I ask.
"Are you kidding? I can't wait to get off this plane; my tuchas (butt) is killing me." We both laughed with excitement.
"I can't wait to breathe the sweet air and feel the warm sun. But, most of all I can't wait to be in Israel, my temple of healing."
Pamela is my mentor and best friend, even though she is eighteen years my senior. She is a brilliant dark haired woman who has spent her life as a professional teacher and paralegal. I used to watch Pamela in awe as she constantly gave her grown children signs of affection, addressing her daughter as "honey" and her son as "sweetheart" and always saying, "I love you" at the end of every phone conversation she had with them. I found a true teacher and friend in Pamela. God

blessed me with her and her teachings; I'm truly grateful for having her in my life.

I first met Pamela in the year 2000, from an ad in the Chicago Tribune. The ad read "Volunteers for Israel," and Pamela was president of the Chicago chapter.

Steve convinced me that I needed to do something to heal my wounds; the years of waking up in the middle of the night in cold sweats, having uncontrolled flashbacks; exhibiting bursts of anger toward people around me, and of course the spontaneous spells of crying were too much to bear any longer. The effects of child abuse always took a toll on my physical, emotional and mental well-being, but as I aged, the stress in reliving the trauma grew more intense. The triggers from my past that haunted my mind and body became harder and harder to disguise.

Israel was always a place I wanted to visit, but the thought of actually going there frightened me. I had many reasons for being fearful of visiting Israel. I had never traveled anywhere by myself and I had always felt uneasy around the Jewish people.

I was lying in bed one day when Steve came in the bedroom with the ad from the Chicago Tribune.

I wasn't much interested in volunteering in Israel or anywhere for that matter. I felt depressed and sad, not to mention I had no desire to even get out of bed let alone go on a trip halfway around the world.

"Holly, here's an ad to volunteer in the Israel army. Why don't you read it and see if this is something you could do?"

"No, I don't want to go there; I just want to stay in bed."

"Holly, you can't live the rest of your life in bed; do something, anything, but get your ass out of bed," Steve demanded.

"Fine!"

I read the newspaper ad and made the call to Pamela. She was so nice and comforting on the phone. Her voice was full of enthusiasm and excitement. I managed to listen to this over-excited woman without being irritated at her passion to sell me on volunteering in Israel for a few weeks. Toward the end of the conversation, I felt a sense of interest and realized I needed to give taking this trip serious thought.

This might be a good experience for me. After all, I am a Jew, and I might even get a chance to learn about my heritage.

Even though my mother didn't teach my sisters or me anything about being a Jew, she was raised Orthodox, and reminded us often that we were Jewish.

Curled up on the sofa with my flannel blanket, I spent the rest of the day and evening thinking about my fear of the Jewish people. My mother's family always seemed to be a loving, kind bunch, but I always felt as though they didn't care for my sisters or me very much. We were not raised Jewish and even though they were pleasant to us on our few visits with them, I always believed they knew about the abuse, and that left me feeling sad.

Two months later, I went on the Volunteers for Israel program, and I met Pamela at the army base. She and I became friends from the first moment we met, and I ended up falling in love with Israel. This was truly my home away from home. For the first time in my life I wasn't scared of life, and I learned from my three-week stint on the army base how to enjoy myself and the company of other people.

After I returned from my trip, I would spend hours on the phone with Pamela. She would teach me about Judaism and sometimes I would travel from the suburbs into the city to visit her.

Pamela and I decided to go back to Israel and volunteer again. We would travel back and forth several times together. In between our volunteering, we chose to become Israeli citizens. I embraced my Jewishness so much that I feared it being taken away from me. I needed something to prove to myself that I belonged, I mattered. I wanted to have something showing my heritage. I was beginning to feel I was really a person who was a part of a people.

Pamela really wanted to move to Israel, and after a few visits together, we made *aliyah*, becoming Israeli citizens. Steve wasn't real keen on the idea, but understood, as I had begun to realize my mother had given me something of so much worth, even though she somehow, along the way lost the importance there is in being a Jew. I felt that value as I needed my spirit to be alive, to learn and feel the ancient scriptures of my ancestors.

Over the course of our trips together, Pamela began teaching me the prayers for *Shabbat* (Sabbath), she taught me about the holidays, the meaning of Hebrew words, the stories of our ancestors, and why it is so important to teach our children about being Jews. Pamela was teaching me how to enrich my life with the riches of being part of a people who have a vast array of history on this earth.

After my fifth visit to Israel, Steve could see how I was coming alive and healing from the pain and effects of the abuse I endured. I was no longer a timid ball of flesh who stayed in my bedroom for fear that the boogie men of the world were out to get me. He saw that Israel was a magical and spiritual place for me. Israel was this powerful force that sucked me in. I wanted to spend more time in Israel to learn the language, and to not let go of the wonderful, alive feeling I had developed.

The air in Israel is like a breath of life, and when I breathe it I feel spiritually alive, an awakening of my true self. I began to embrace the fact that I am just as human as any human; that I mattered just as much as any person matters. I began learning how to be me.

Steve and I agreed I would spend three months in Israel learning the language and working there to support myself. But more importantly, I would find healing in a profoundly spiritual way by embracing myself for who I am and what I was born as, a Jew. I needed to do this journey to save my life from my own self-destruction.

Pamela and I decided to go to school together in Tel Aviv to learn Hebrew. She was making her plans to move to Israel and I was learning how to trust people by opening myself up and slowly talking about the abuse I endured.

We rented a run-down apartment above an art gallery owned by one of Pamela's friends, an older man named Ephraim, who lived on the top floor with his wife.

"Keep your seatbelts fastened and cell phones off until the plane has come to a complete stop and the seatbelt sign is off," the flight attendant announced as the plane began its descent. The plane landed and drove on the landing strip as people unbuckled their seatbelts and immediately started talking on their cell phones. Pamela and I looked around and laughed.

"Well, this *is* Israel," Pamela said with a laugh.

Walking down the steps of the plane, and into the humid air, I could feel my hair curl up in ringlets. I couldn't help but smile as I breathed in the sweetness of the air.

Catching a taxi from the airport, we had the driver drop us off at our crappy, cockroach-ridden apartment above the art gallery. We entered the concrete-walled apartment exhausted and excited.

"We finally made it", I said, throwing my bags onto the speckled linoleum floor in the living room.

"I want to get everything put away then take a shower," Pamela said with a sigh. "I want to go to the kabbalat Shabbat at Eshet tonight and hear Navone sing." Pamela loved going to hear Navone sing at a local pub around the corner.

We put our belongings away and Pamela jumped in the shower. I decided to walk around the busy streets. I headed out on Gordon Street to see Ephraim. I often called Ephraim "Abba," which is Hebrew for father. Even though I've never known what it was like to have a loving father, my visits with Ephraim always left me feeling as though I had enjoyed the company of family.

After the nice Shabbat weekend, Pamela and I headed off to school. We walked down Ben Yehuda Street and stopped at a local kiosk for a quick bagel to eat during break.

"I'm a nervous wreck. Every attempt I've ever made at school failed," I said, taking a heaping bite out of my gigantic bagel.

"Don't worry about it," Pamela reassured me. "You'll do fine. You're one of the smartest people I know."

Pamela never judges me; she only encourages me, even when I think of myself as a lost cause.

Walking into the school together we found our classroom and sat next to each other. We both knew this was going to be an experience neither one of us would ever forget.

"Ma shlomcha? Ma shlomach?" the teacher asked.

I pulled out my pad of paper and wrote down what the teacher said. *Great, what the heck was that?* "I'm gonna to flunk," I said, pouting, "I just know it."

Later, as always, Pamela comforted me with her words of wisdom and knowledge. "Don't worry, you'll do great," she whispered. "You'll help me and I'll help you."

"I thought our first day of class went great, didn't you?" Pamela asked as we left school and headed back to the apartment.

"Yeah, too bad I didn't understand a word the teacher said", I said, pulling a green apple out of my black book bag. I was famished and concerned about my abilities to concentrate. I can never concentrate, another misfortune of having PTSD. But I was ready to learn and willing to try.

"We need to go to the beach every day after school. There is always peace and tranquility at the beach, and you can smell the sweetness in the air that you love so much from the sea," Pamela said, shoving her notebook back into her black canvas bag.

Every day after school, Pamela and I headed over to the beach. Sometimes we did our homework; other times we would just lie in the sand, soaking up the sun and smelling the sweet air that emanated from the sea. It was there at the sea I would feel safe enough to share with Pamela my horrid stories of childhood abuse.

Cleaning the apartment was always a chore; I cleaned the bathroom and Pamela cleaned the kitchen. It made no difference how hard we scrubbed; the apartment never seemed clean enough. If it were possible to buy a box of elbow grease at the local supermarket we would have paid any price for it.

"Where do I put my clothes to dry?" I asked hand-washing my clothes in a bucket.

"There's a clothesline out on the porch."

I grabbed the purple plastic bucket full of fresh smelling, rung-out clothes, and headed out onto the porch off the kitchen. I wiped down the clothesline with a wet towel and noticed the black soot that ended up on the wet rag. *Good thing I wiped that down.*

Placing each item on the line one by one, I fixated my eye on a red thread running through the white clothes line. I shook my head, finished my task, and with three pins still in my hand, reached down to grab the bucket when a movie from the past suddenly entered my mind. No warning, just out of the blue the movie flashed in and out, then back in, replaying the past. I dropped the bucket and turned to look back at the red thread in the clothesline. It appeared to be torn and tattered, not at all the clothesline I had just placed my clothes on. Stepping back, I stared as my mind relived the horrible event.

*   *   *

The Memory…

The year is 1974 and I'm sitting in my bedroom looking out the window on this nice summer day, watching cars drive by on the interstate. The window is open, and the smell of exhaust is in the air. I like this; quiet and peaceful. My father isn't home and there's no chaos, no yelling and no screaming, but most of all no beatings. Mom's downstairs and I'm in here happy and content, just watching and thinking about God, wondering if there's a God. I've never given God much thought before, but now I want to believe in God, because I pray to God all the time, so there must be a God. I wish for God to make all days just like this day, peaceful, no loud screaming, only calm.

A sound from below blares into the calmness. It's my father pulling onto the gravel drive with a red horse trailer behind his beat up mustard colored Chevrolet Corvair. *I wonder if there's a horse inside the trailer?* I gasp with excitement and run down the curved staircase, yelling, "Dad is home with a horse!"

I run into the kitchen, passing my mother and Barbra. I run straight out the back door, jumping off the back porch steps onto the sidewalk where I squash at least three night crawlers who came out with the heavy rain from the night before. I'm so excited to see the horse! I run up to my father. "Can I see? Can I see the horse?" I beg, my hands folded together.

"There's no horse in there. I'm taking your sister to the farm to go horseback riding." He unlatches the trailer from the ugly, beat up car.

"Can I come?"

"No! Now get your ass back in the house and help your mother cook dinner," he barks.

Help my mother cook, yuck, I want to go to the farm and see the horses. I don't want to cook, that's boring.

"Please, can I go?" I plead.

"No, damnit! Now get your ass back in the house and tell your sister to get her fat ass out here. I don't have all fuckin day." He's raised his voice and gone red in the face.

Now I'm really upset. I really want to go, but I sense I'm making him mad. With my hands clenched into fists, I decide to push the issue, hoping that he'll get sick of my behavior and take me along. Unfortunately, I have no idea what's in store for me for not obeying. I know there's a possibly of a spanking with the belt, but I don't care. I really want to go, even if it's just to watch Barbra ride the pretty horses.

"Can I please go?" I ask with a pleading heart.

"Fucking stupid little bitch!" he yells. "You just don't know how to listen. What the fuck is wrong with you?"

I'm very used to being called nasty names; the bad language and name-calling just seem to bounce off me. I'm mad and I want to go. I'm determined to make him take me.

Running toward the back yard I'm going to do something I've never done before. I'm going to act out. *That'll show him.*

I run to the back porch, stomping on those night crawlers I previously killed as if to kill them even more and march straight up the stairs, pounding my feet with every step I take. I'm crying, mad and hurt. I want everyone to know of my injustice. Racing through the kitchen, up the curved staircase and into Barbra's room, I grab a magazine she's been working on. It's a magazine full of pictures of different horses that she's compiled. I take her magazine and rip it into shreds page by page. I'm so angry I can't go see the horses, and I know she doesn't want to go. He always makes her go, and besides, all he does is yell and hit her and call her bad names. But I want to go! I want to see the horses even if it includes being slapped in the back of my head and called names. I don't care; I want to see those horses!

Barbra comes running up the stairs and sees what I've done. I'm so upset that I didn't hear her come up the stairs. I only hear the gasping of her breath as she stands in the doorway of her bedroom.

"What have you done, you little brat?" she screams.

"You always get to go and I don't! It's not fair, it's not fair, Barbra. I want to go and you hate going. It's not fair. I'm old enough to go. I'm nine now! I'm old enough to go!" I scream.

My father comes up the stairs. I throw the torn pages of the homemade horse magazine to the floor and run to my room. I slide under my bed as if I'm a professional baseball player that just slid into home base. Now I'm terrified he'll find me. I peek out from under the pink blanket draped over my bed. *I hope he doesn't find me.* I stop crying and begin praying to my newly found God that he'll leave.

Please let him leave; please let him leave, I pray. I pray that my sister won't tell Daddy what I have just done. But of course she'll have to. She has no choice—he sees the paper on the floor. He starts shouting at her.

"What the fuck happened here?" he roars.

I know she'll have to tell him the truth in order to save herself from his wrath.

"Holly did it," she says, her voice shaking.

I'm very quiet under my bed, covering my mouth with my tiny hands, hoping and praying he'll just leave. Then I open my eyes and there he is, looking right at me. His words are like fire, he's so furious.

"Get out from that bed, NOW!" he shouts with intense fire in his throat, a red vein popping on his forehead. I swallow hard scooting my way out from under my bed. He reaches down, grabbing and jerking my arm, dragging me out. I feel like I'm going to pee in my pants, I'm so petrified. With one hand on my arm, he reaches down and grabs the back of my hair. Jerking me up, he turns his dry, dark, piercing gaze into my tortured eyes, and with his hissing lips he spits,

"You are nothing more than a fucking dog."

I glance over at Barbra, who's watching the scene from my bedroom doorway, biting her fingernails. I tightly close my eyes, wishing I had never touched her magazine.

"Because you are a dog, you will be treated like a dog," he says in his fire-throwing voice. He drags me down the curved stairs with my hair still in his iron grip. We land on the bottom step and turn the corner through the bathroom into the threshold of the kitchen, Barbra following behind.

"Here comes the dog!" he yells, spit spraying from his teeth. He pulls me into the kitchen where my mother is cooking. He stops, shakes my head from side to side by my hair and tells me again with his face close to my cheek, "This is where you need to be, learning how to cook, not acting like the dog that you are."

Tears stream down my face as I stand terrified, while my insides feel like a shake mixer and my blood vibrates through my veins. My eyes are blurry from my frightened tears, but I try really hard to hold back any sounds that might come from my mouth. I see my mother standing over the sink and Marcia leaning on a barstool as I begin to whimper from holding back the fear. I know any sound will only intensify the situation and make him more outraged, so I hold both my hands over my mouth, trying to muffle my whimpers with my tiny palms.

Still holding on to the back of my hair, he drags me out the back door, from the kitchen onto the porch. He pushes me forward down the four wooden stairs as my arms land on the squashed night crawlers.

"Get over to the middle of the clothesline, dog!" he hollers with rage.

I still don't want to make a sound. I wipe the snot from my nose with my wrist and swipe at my eyes with my tiny fingers. I walk briskly over to the middle of the clothesline. Walking slow will only make matters worse, and I know he can explode at any time.

My father takes apart one of the two clotheslines that are stretched out from pole to pole while I stand shaking, looking on as the cars pass by.

"Sit your ass down, dog," he shouts.

I do as he demands. Looking at the back of the house, I see my sisters and mother watching me through the kitchen window. *Why does he want me out here? What are his plans for me in this backyard?*

"You want to act like a dog? You will be treated like a dog," he says, tying the clothesline in front of me.

He kneels down and grabs my wrists, putting them together. He ties the clothesline around them, then puts my feet together and ties the clothesline to my ankles. He ties a noose around my neck, and from that he ties the end of the line to the remaining line connected to the two poles.

"Dog, you have room to run back and forth. You are not to leave or have your mother untie you while I'm away," he shrieks, walking off through the yard, whistling for Barbra to get out of the house and into the car.

I really hope no one sees me out here like this; I know they'll make fun of me. I can do nothing. I have no idea how long he's going to be gone. I swallow hard; praying to God, *Please make me disappear. I just wish to disappear, please.*

I wipe the rest of my tears away with my fingers and look down toward the grass. I notice a ladybug crawling on a blade of grass. I begin to talk to it as it travels from one blade of grass to the next, then I notice some yucky stuff in my hair.

"Ewww, night crawler guts, how nasty, how'd that get in my hair?" Bending my head down to my hands I began picking the worm guts from my hair.

I hunch my back, knees up to my chest, wrapping my arms around my legs. Rocking back and forth until the day turns to night. I dissociate into a make believe world that feels safe, as thoughts of dancing and singing take over my consciousness.

It starts to rain. Catching a few raindrops on my eyelashes I wake from my trance. I look up at the back of the house to see if my mother will tell me I can come in, but she doesn't. I'm so tired from sitting out here in this grass, as raindrops bounce off my face and arms. All tied up and wet, I start to cry burying my head between my knees. My back hurts from sitting in this hunched over position for so long, and I'm hungry.

I make a brave attempt to yell for my mother.

"Mom! Mom?"

She doesn't hear me, but I don't stop. I have nothing to lose. Finally, my mother comes out, holding the screen door with one hand.

"What is it? You know I can't let you in the house. Your father told you to stay out here until he comes home."
"Please? It's raining. I'm cold and wet. Please, can you just explain to him?" I plead.
"See if you can walk over to the steps."
The back porch has a roof, and if I can stretch the clothesline over to the steps, I can get shelter from the rain. I now have permission to move. My father may have said I have room to move back and forth, but I know better than to leave the spot he sat me down in. It's the way it is, he might say he never told me I can move and then I'll get all scared and he'll laugh, saying he's joking. The clothesline reaches the step with a little stretching. I'm happy now; I'm out of the rain. I wanna eat now, but mom went back inside. Looking up into the kitchen window I can see my mother standing next to the table making a plate of food for Marcia.
"Can I have some?" I scream.
"Did your father say you could have dinner?" she asks, opening the door.
"He didn't say."
"Fine." She turns around; the door slams shut.
I'm lucky, I think. *I get to eat dinner, ha, ha, ha, he won't know.* Mom opens the door and hands me a plate of food. I eat while watching the rainfall from the darkening, cloudy sky. I finish my plate and yell from the porch again, asking her to wash my plate. Just in case, I want to leave no signs of eating. I never know what mood he'll come home in, and I don't want to risk more punishment.
I close my eyes and listen as the rain hits the puddles on the sidewalk. Eventually I fall asleep, ending my punishment.

*   *   *

This story is an example of "Betrayal Bond." My mother becomes my hero for allowing me to sit under the roof of the porch while providing me with food. Because my abusers are also my parents, the very people responsible for my daily care, I mentally minimize the abuse they inflict on me by making them out to be my heroes. This is how I survive.

*   *   *

Healing — 2004

"What happened to me?" I ask my therapist, years later. "What happened to my soul, my being?" I ask her sitting in her office, feeling sad and ashamed. "What happened to you, Holly?" she asks.

"I felt humiliated, I live with the guilt of not being worthy.

I live my life thinking I'm less than human. I'm the equivalent of a dog." Tears are filling my eyes.

"I live my life surviving it. You know people drove by the backyard. Those people who drove by saw me tied up to that clothesline. They did nothing! My mother did nothing! We lived close to my father's family, they never did anything. My aunt, my uncles, my grandmother, they all lived there in the same town, and they knew he was an alcoholic monster. They saw him beat us. They saw him scream vulgar names at us. They saw how he hurt us, and they saw how my mother didn't protect us. They knew. They were always around. My father's family came to our house every holiday. He would often drop us off at grandma's house. How I hated going to grandma's house. We would play with her inbred poodles that were mean."

"What were they so afraid of?" I asked.

"What do you think they were they afraid of Holly?" My therapist asks, sitting back in her oversized lime green chair.

"Him…I never saw him beat any of his family, I never saw him whip out his brown thick leather belt and beat them in the head, or their backs or, their arms or their butt, or their legs or their faces. But it was perfectly okay for them to see a child hit in the face, or the head or the butt, back, legs and arms. Yeah, that's fine, watch the show of abuse and then don't do a freaking thing about it! You know my mother was never beaten as a child?"

Taking a breath I look across at my therapist. Her eyes are droopy and her mouth is pouting.

"My mother would say, 'I don't know from that.' I guess she thought because she didn't know from that it was perfectly fine to beat her kids, it was perfectly fine to tell them they are dogs, sluts, worthless fucking bitches, and it is perfectly fine to tie your small, child up to a clothesline and tell her she's a *fucking dog.*" My rage is boiling over.

"She had a nice family. She was treated with respect and dignity, and her family would never tolerate such vitriolic treatment." I envied my mother, I realized.

"So what the hell was she so afraid of? Watching child abuse and doing *nothing* is not okay. When will the American people understand that protecting the assholes who harm children is *not fucking okay*? So what were they so afraid of? That they could think it was all right for a small child to be treated that way?

"I'll tell you what they're afraid of, they're afraid of pissing him off. They were afraid of losing their relationship with him. They're afraid *he* wouldn't talk to them anymore. They're *afraid* of stirring the family pot. Did they really think they meant that much to this alcoholic creep? Let's see, how did his words go? 'You're a fucking dog' and did his actions of tying me up to a clothesline affect me?" I was asking my therapist and myself.

Blinking the tears away, I look over at a box of tissue sitting on a round table next to my chair.

"Well, it left me with the thought that I was not human, therefore I didn't connect to humans. I didn't connect to anyone. Oh sure, I went through life putting on a disguise, but spent thousands of nights crying and sobbing for thinking I was a *dog.*

I connected to our family pet, Tina, she was the family *dog*, although the poor thing would get beaten, too. My father didn't care who he beat. He would beat anything; as long as it was breathing, and smaller and weaker than him, he would strike against it."

"What could Mom have done differently?" my therapist asks.

"Mom had a skill, a way to support herself. She also had a supportive family, she could have turned to, which she did, and they helped, but she would always go back to him. She *could* have left the a-hole for good, which would have been a smart choice. It wouldn't have mattered to me if we ended up living in a shelter; anything would have been better than living with that crazy monster. Mom could have called the police and pressed charges against him, that would have helped; if anything it would have sent me the message she cared."

"Did your mother ever call the police?"

"What? No she never called the police; she protected Dad. If the neighbors called the police because of the screams that emanated from the house or the back yard, the police would come and realize it was a 'family matter' and turn around in the drive way. This was Omaha, Nebraska, the little conservative town. The police never bothered. Omaha is an ideal place to raise a family."

"How does that make you feel?"

"It makes me feel angry as hell," I said. "America is full of 'turning the other cheek' per se, but it's sad they don't read the Bible where it says, 'It is forbidden to stand by and do nothing.'"

"Would you like to put dad in a chair and tell him how calling you a dog made you feel, how it affected your life?"

"Sure, put the asshole in the chair. I have a few things I need to say to him."

My therapist pulls out a wooden folding chair and opens it up. She moves the chair in different places throughout the room, far away from me and near me.

"Ok, your dad is in the chair. He can't harm you."

I look at the chair and imagine him sitting there. I become frightened, while taking deep breaths.

"It's alright, Holly, he can't hurt you. Do you want me to move the chair farther away?" she asks while I look into her hazel eyes.

"No, move him closer. I want to be face to face. I want him to hear what I have to say. I want to project my anger straight at him, not from the side."

Taking a deep breath I stare at the empty chair for approximately fifteen to twenty minutes, I begin imagining my father's face; smiling at me, laughing at me.

"How could you call your daughter a dog?" I ask in a shaky voice.

Imagining him still smiling, laughing at me, makes me feel unworthy again, and scared.

"How does Dad make you feel, Holly?" my therapist asks again.

"Terrified!" I tell her, tears drop from my eyes. I keep looking at the chair. I can't speak. I feel paralyzed, remembering the sting in the painful words of calling me a "dog." I feel empty and lonely. I want to run out of her office and find a small hiding place. I wish for a small crack in the concrete I can crawl into and hide, where no one will find me, especially him.

He's still laughing at me, smiling with his big white teeth. His eyes are like dark daggers full of hate and rage. I suddenly feel this urge to jump up and smack the shit out of him.

"Stop laughing at me you fucking prick," I yell, standing from the chair, while smacking his imaginary face.

"How dare you treat me like a dog! I'm *not* a fucking dog. I'm a human being. I said to stop laughing at me, you fucking freak!

"You're an asshole you know that, a worthless piece of shit that had *no* business having children. *You* don't deserve children, and you're a twisted, horrible *father*! I fucking hate you!

"I fucking hate your guts. You are the lowest form of life that exists on this planet. *You're an abuser*, Fucker!"

I feel the rage inside bubble toward my throat.

"Let me tell you something, you piece of vile shit. I am *better* than you. I am *better* than you will *ever* be in your life. You are a loser, and you had *no* right to hurt me. You had *no* right to treat me like I was put on this earth to be your personal punching bag. You had *no* right to tie me up to that fucking clothesline, and you had *no* right to call me a *fucking dog*, you loser!!" I holler, pacing the green-carpeted floor in front of the chair.

"How are you feeling, Holly?" my therapist asks quietly.

"*Better*. I'm still angry." I respond pacing, staring at the chair; visualizing his big teeth smiling. "I'm not done."

"You think you can just sit there and laugh at me. You think you can just smile as if I don't matter. Well, I got news for you asshole, I do matter, and I do have a voice. You should be sitting in a jail cell for what you did to me and my sisters."

Taking another deep breath I continue to pace the carpet, my hands behind my back.

"How does it feel to be helpless sitting there knowing you can't defend yourself? Huh asshole? How does it feel? That is how you made me feel. I was helpless. I was a small child, you fucking bully. Guess what, asshole? Father's Day is coming up and I think you deserve a bit of thanks. Thanks for the fucking PTSD, Dad! I couldn't have developed it without all your wonderful help.

"Thanks for the years of not connecting to other people or life, Dad! Thanks for the miserable life you gave me, Dad! Aren't you proud? Aren't you proud of what a *bad* father you were? Are? Aren't you proud you infested your daughters with thinking they were sluts even before we knew what the fucking definition of a *slut* was, Dad? What kind of parents call up their children and tell them they just can't ever talk to their children ever again? Well, I've got news for you Dad, you assholes did me a huge favor by cutting off contact, because now Dad I've been able to heal. I can now see and feel you for what you really are, a child abuser. Thirty-three years I've put up with your friggin abuse, thirty-three years! Well, no more, oh sure the physical abuse may have stopped when I was nineteen or twenty, but even then you beat the shit out of me and I was fucking eight months pregnant with my daughter." Grabbing a tissue I wipe my nose.

"You act as though you and Mom were *good* parents. Well, I have news for you, the both of you fuckers were *bad, rotten, awful pieces of shit parents that had no business having children!* I will never ever forgive you! NEVER! Now instead I strive for Shlemut," I said, opening my arms.

"Oh, you don't know what *Shlemut* is, *Dad*? Well I'll tell you, fucker. It is a Hebrew term us Jews use to find peace and a life full of happiness and wholesomeness without giving fuckers like you forgiveness! Now I'm done with you! Go live your miserable life with that stupid woman you turned into an abuser. I'll deal with her later. Now get the fuck out!" I scream, as I pop the chair closed.

Taking a seat, my therapist asks, "How do you feel, Holly?"

"I feel sad," I say bending over in anguish, weeping from my pain. "No child should ever have to go through this, *no one*. This is awful. I hate this. I hate having to fix what they've broken. I hate going through this aching, throbbing, stinging pain and knowing I have parents who hate their children," I say with my head in my lap.

"I'm going to go home now and sit with my pain, I need to really be with myself and feel my pain alone," I said, rising to my feet. Still feeling the anguish thrumming through me, I turn to my therapist and ask, "Who was that French writer who spoke of disguise? Oh yes, Francois de La Rochefoucauld." I reach toward the round table, grab a tissue and wiping my nose, I swallow, "He once wrote, 'We are so accustomed to disguise ourselves to others that in the end we become disguised to ourselves.' Well, that's exactly what happened to me isn't it? But no more, I refuse to live in disguise any longer."

* * *

Shlemut
The Hebrew word "Shlemut" simply means completeness.

Since we are not always able to forgive our wrongdoers or abusers, we can't continue to live life with rage, fear, anger and self-destruction. *Shlemut* gives us the ability to strive for a life of peace. Judaism's concept of *shlemut* gives a victim a feeling of wholeness and peace along with a sense of unity and personal integrity and growth, without having to give "forgiveness" to those who harm us.

Seeking *shlemut* for myself has helped me find my way to recovery, along with experiencing my goal of living a life of wholeness. Simply put, shalom equals peace and peace equals *shlemut*.

Chapter 5

The Refrigerator

The Trigger —2003

The house was full of chaos. The kids were getting ready for school and the three neighbor boys, Chuck, Mark, and Sam, all eleven-year-olds, have just arrived to spend their half-hour before school playing with my younger sons, Scott, also eleven and Stephen, my nine-year-old. Sean my eldest child is twenty-two and lives on his own in Nebraska and my daughter Shana, who's nineteen, has just moved into her first apartment, which is thirty minutes away.

Steve's in the kitchen throwing dried cereal in bowls for the kids and I'm stuffing snacks and books into their backpacks. The five boys run around the house in circles from the living room, through the dining room, into the kitchen, back around into the family room. Playing tag and screaming back and forth to each other. "You're it!"

Honey, the family schnauzer, runs behind the kids, barking, fervently trying to grab their socks, while smashing into the laundry room wall, spilling her water dish. The fifteen-pound little snot manages to drag a trail of water through the kitchen, which I just know I'll slip on at some point today. I know the house will quiet down soon so I tell myself to calm down before the onset of an anxiety attack enters my nervous system. I decide to start my day by hitting the grocery store, and as I sit down at the oak table to make my list, Steve tells me what he needs from the store, while the boys put in their two cents about what snacks I need to buy: cookies, Rice Crispy treats, and squishy, fruit-bursting, pop-in-the-mouth, full–of-vitamin-C gummy balls.

It's 9 a.m. and the kids blow out the door yelling, "Love you, Mom!"

Steve blows me a kiss while slamming the garage door shut, and I look down at the wet-footed pooch that's sitting next to my leg, looking up at me, as if to say, "Where'd all the fun go?"

Gathering my things together, I grab my black leather purse and car keys and head out the door to start my trip to the grocery store.

Filling my basket, I remember my husband's hygiene list: shaving cream, contact solution, and razors. Somehow, I just know the longer I look at the different types of razor packages, the more confused I'll get. Regardless, I know whatever kind I choose it will be the wrong kind, and since I frustrate easily, I don't delay. I pick one type of razor and hope for the best, throwing it into the shopping cart as I head for the next aisle.

I make my way from one aisle to the next, pushing my heavy, rickety cart. I feel the anger in my head ready to take over as I push my uncooperative cart.

I've always felt my anger escalate at any little thing in my life. I know it's all because I haven't released the anger I feel inside about those who hurt me as a child. The years of rage that have been sitting dormant inside my body are now leaking out in tiny bits on things or people. Logically I know these things or people have nothing to do with why I'm really feeling angry, but my emotions of extreme annoyance overshadow my logic and I irrationally strike out. This type of behavior often scares me as I recognize my father's tongue in my temper.

Fighting with a heavy, non-cooperative shopping cart that has a sticky wheel, I somehow gather the strength to not get pissed off and push the cart into a display of food. Instead I shove the poorly constructed cart into a checkout lane.

With a frown on my face, I notice a magazine that reads in big bold print on the cover, "Successful Exercising Tip." Somehow I take this ad as a personal attack against myself and feel even angrier at the world. Grabbing the magazine I throw it on the conveyer belt, vowing to write a nasty letter to the editor.

Walking out to my car while pushing the stubborn cart, a store employee who is walking into the store, stops and asks me if I need help.

"Of course I need help, this cart is awful," I exclaim.

"Here let me push it." The young man says as he grabs hold of the bar and pushes the cart out to my van.

As I hit the button on my keychain, the van doors unlock and I open the driver's door, throwing my purse on the seat.

The tall, dark-haired young man loads my bags of groceries into the back of the van and I help by tossing in the last couple of sacks. Unexpectedly, he reached up to pull the back door down to close it! My reflexes caused me to jump back with a startled gasp!

"Gee ma'am I wasn't gonna hit ya, I just wanted to shut the back lid."

"Yeah, I knew that, thanks for your help." Swallowing hard with embarrassment I shuffle over to the driver's door and get in. *Damnit, you have to stop that friggin flinching, it's so humiliating, stop flinching, Holly, just stop, grrrrr.*

Driving home, I feel my head overheat at the rage I feel at myself for flinching, and the supermarket for not fixing that rotten shopping cart. I dig in my purse for my

Pepto-Bismol tablets. In fact I feel very upset at this point and start thinking absurd thoughts, as I believe the world is out to get me by making my life harder to live.

Pulling my mini-van into the garage, I get out of the car and somehow manage to carry in all my bags without letting the dog out of the house. I've made that mistake too many times to count, and it is a mistake I have been known to take out on the poor dog.

Filling my refrigerator and cabinets with food, I try really hard to calm myself by taking extra deep breaths. But that calmness soon comes to an end when I gather and scrunch up the grocery store plastic bags that are really pissing me off for spilling out of the cabinet and falling all around me. I throw the bags on the floor and stand up from my squatting position to close the open refrigerator. I stare at the fully stocked fridge, while my eyes fixate on a bottle of Tabasco sauce. *I don't recall buying a bottle of Tabasco sauce,* I thought, as I looked intently at this slim little bottle with red and green labeling.

What the fuck is that bottle doing in there?

The doors to the refrigerator and freezer are wide open as my mind recalls the memory of Tabasco sauce. My head starts to feel very hot and my body tenses as I begin to sweat. Taking a hard swallow, I blink real hard and feel my anger turn into fear as my hands form into fists. I can feel the effects of my PTSD firing missiles from my brain to my body, as the kitchen closes in around me.

I then feel a stream of wetness run down my face as I back away from the refrigerator, hitting the counter with my back. Swallowing hard again, I feel the heat from my face swell up into my cheeks. I shake my head, pulling down on my hair by my ears. I pound my fist into the top of my head. I then reach over to the kitchen sink and turn on the cold water, slapping the water onto my face.

"Push it away Holly, you stupid girl, push it away," I scream. I look up from the kitchen window as my memory takes hold of me, showing me when I was this tiny little nine-year-old swinging on the tire swing in my parents' backyard.

*   *   *

The Memory....

Playing in the backyard with Marcia on the tire swing, Barbra, who's now 15-years-old, comes walking out of the house across the yard toward us. I know she didn't come to play with us; she looks to be in a bad mood.

"Where're ya going?" I ask while standing on the tire swing, swaying back and forth.

"I'm not telling you brats anything," Barbra hissed; smoke forming around her mouth from the crisp air, as she marched through the neighbor's back yard.

She doesn't like Marcia and me very much. I figure she just thinks of us as pests, and she really hates it if she has to baby-sit us.

My father is in the house watching football. That's all he does these days, sit around watching football and drinking his beer. Marcia and I know it's better to stay outside. The thought of getting beat for running in front of the television is an experience we've shared many times before and tend to avoid.

My mom's working now, so we have to stay home with him all the time. This makes for an uncomfortable setting for Barbra, because she hates dad a lot. She always leaves the house before his football team loses the game.

Just as the neighbor kids come over to play on the tire swing with us, my father whistles for us to come in. We're dogs, so the whistling means to come. Like always, we serve to please, as all dogs do. Marcia and I jump off the swing, running across the tall grass that has grown in the backyard. We run up the steps, right up to the back door. We always try to make record time. As we enter, we see our father standing in the kitchen next to the speckled lime green counter top. We both know not to speak until spoken to.

He tells us he's hungry, and since we've been watching mom cook we have to prepare him lunch according to his explicit instructions: two pieces of toast cut into squares, put into a cereal bowl, salted and peppered, with milk poured on top and a side dish of hard-boiled eggs. Before leaving us to our new task, he reminds us not to disturb him in the family room as the football game's on today. Marcia and I look at each other without saying a word. We feel each other's fear and our own, as neither of us has ever cooked anything before. I guess since I'm ten and Marcia's eight, he thinks we know what to do.

"How are we going to cook this? You haven't cooked before; whatcha gonna do?" Marcia asks with serious concern.

"Don'tcha think I know that?" I whisper. "I don't know, but we're gonna have to try or we'll get in trouble."

I've spent many hours in the kitchen watching my mother cook. My father reminds me often that I need to learn to cook and clean so I know how to be a good wife like my mother if I'm to ever have a husband. *How can we prepare this meal the same way my mother prepares food?* I feel like crying, but that's not an option.

Feeling crazed, I tell Marcia to get the milk and eggs from the refrigerator, while I grab a pan from the cabinet, filling it with water and carrying it to the cook top slowly so I don't spill any of the water. I know this lunch needs to be prepared quickly or things will get ugly for me. I turn the stove knob to high, light the match from the matchbox on the green counter and throw it in the burner. Though I'm scared to death, I make the fire without much trouble.

"Marcia, grab the milk from the fridge and place it on the counter then go back for the eggs."

Marcia goes in the fridge and grabs a few eggs. Of course she drops one, and it splatters on the floor. I grab the eggs from her as she retrieves a dishrag to clean up the mess. I begin to panic again; *I don't know how many to boil because he didn't tell me and we can't interrupt him.*

What am I to do? I have no choice but to guess. I choose five eggs. I put the eggs in the pot one egg at a time and as I do the water begins to overflow, spilling onto the cook top. It's very clear I'm not cut out to do this task, but what choice do I have? I grab a cup and drop it into the already boiling water. It's very hot. Just as I pull the cup out of the water, I hear my father scream, "Where's my lunch?"

I immediately jump. My eyes grow big with fear and my hands began to sweat. I glance over at Marcia; she looks as though she's going to pee her pants and cry.

"This is not good," I tell her.

"I'm scared," she says, "I want to go back outside, I don't want to cook. I'm scared."

The situation keeps getting worse and I feel as though we're moving in slow motion. I'm so terrified and nervous, I yell at Marcia, "Just get the bread ready to toast, put it in the toaster and push the button down." Marcia's body begins to shake as she nervously puts the bread in the toaster.

I fix the water problem in the pan to fit all five eggs. I wipe my little hands off from the boiling water that splattered me, and then realize I have no idea how long to cook the eggs, and the water is really bubbling now.

No matter what happens, I know I'm going to be in trouble. This job is much too hard for me and I know it. My mind is on overdrive, so I have no time to think about anything other than getting this meal done. But I still don't know how long to cook the eggs. I make an attempt to silently go into the family room to ask my father how long I need to cook the eggs. Petrified to death, I walk very quietly through the dining room, entering the family room threshold. I look back at Marcia, who's still standing next to the counter; she has a ghostly look on her face and her eyebrows are raised. Her eyes are large like saucers. This of course horrifies me, as the anxiety inside my stomach intensifies.

"What the fuck are you doing?"

I jump as though I just jumped out of my own body, while my brain feels like it's floating to the ceiling. Panicking and filled with terror, I blurt out, "I need to know how long to cook the eggs," I ask in a panicked tone.

"What the fuck is wrong with you? Are you fucking stupid? Bring me my lunch before I come over there and knock your fucking head off your fucking your neck," He responds as his face turns bright red with anger and his eyes darken with a wicked glare.

I run back across the dining room as fast as I can, into the kitchen and right up to the toaster. I grab a butter knife from the drawer and take the toast out of the toaster, grabbing the two hot pieces of toast, and lay them on the counter to be cut. I look over at Marcia, who's still shaking and wide-eyed.

"Do something", I whisper, quivering.

The longer Marcia stands there not doing anything to help me prepare the meal the angrier I get.

"GO! GO! GO!" he yells.

I jump again, and then I realize he's yelling at the television. He yells at the television all the time. He yells and snaps his fingers together at the football games.

Throwing the cut toast into the cereal bowl, I tell Marcia to put salt and pepper on it—lots of pepper I tell her, he likes things hot. She doesn't move and I become furious. I walked over to her, grabbing her by the arm, put the salt and pepper shakers in front of her and whispered, "Salt and pepper the fucking toast."

She starts crying but she knows not to make a sound. I run over to the cook top and turn off the heat. I grab the hot pad and very slowly and carefully take it to the sink. It's a painstaking walk and I have to be slow and careful, not an easy task when I'm under the pressure of my crazed lunatic father.

I pour the water into the sink. Marcia's calm and is no longer crying. I tell her that now she must pour the milk over the toast.

"How much?"

I turn the cold water on and put the eggs under the running water. I go over to Marcia and pour the milk into the cereal bowl.

"Halfway," I tell her, though I'm not real sure. Marcia pulls out a fork from the drawer and sticks it into the bowl; this part of the meal was ready.

"Where the fuck is my food?" he shouts.

I look at Marcia and tell her to take him the toast mixture.

"No! You do it," she pleads while looking up at me, with her sad, big hazel eyes.

"I can't, I have to peel the eggs," I murmur as I place the bowl into the palms of her hands.

"Go, Go, Go!" he screams at the TV again.

Her face a ghastly white, she heads for the dining room. I know she's scared, and afraid she'll fall with the bowl in her hands; that's what fear feels like. I go over to the sink and shut off the cold running water. I grab the eggs that are now cool and easy to handle, I peel them one by one. But they aren't peeling so easy, and they don't look like my mother's eggs.

I have no time to worry about the eggs. I take another bowl from the cabinet and put my lumpy-looking eggs into the new bowl. Marcia runs back into the kitchen as if she had just won a thousand bucks. Her face is no longer white and she is smiling. I begin to feel relief. I let out a big sigh and grab the bowl that contains my lumpy eggs and the salt and pepper shakers. I head toward the family room thinking, *I hope he likes the eggs.*

I enter the family room cautiously, with my head down. I hand my father the bowl of lumpy hard-boiled eggs.

"What...what the fuck happened?"

I slowly look up at his fire blazing eyes.

"Well," I respond with a tremble, "that's just how they turned out."

"Get the fuck out of here; can't you see I'm watching the ball game? What the fuck is wrong with you?"

Feeling full of shame, I slowly walk back into the kitchen. I'm not feeling the same excitement Marcia felt only moments ago. In fact, I feel pretty disappointed and sad. With my head held low and my long brown curly hair in my face, I look around the kitchen for Marcia, who's no longer here. I look out the window and notice she has gone back out to play. I feel like crying. I want to cry because my father is happy at Marcia's accomplishment of the toast and milk course, but I feel rejected and shame. I always get that feeling, and each and every time it hurts like a knife in my heart. I have no idea why the eggs turned lumpy, but what I do know is that I failed my chore.

In the kitchen staring out the window at my sister and her friends playing, I'm startled as my father yells and snaps his fingers at the television. Jumping from his sudden screams at the television, I decide to clean the mess in the kitchen. I was taught how to wash dishes at the age of seven because I'm learning how to be a wife for someone someday. *If I'm good enough, that is,* even though making it to adulthood is something I never think about. I start cleaning, putting the heavy metal toaster back in the corner on the counter, wiping the bread crumbs off the counter with my wet wash cloth. My father screams for me to come into the family room, and, as usual, he calls out my name along with my sisters' names until he calls out to the one he really wants, and it's me he wants. Feeling sad and rejected, I walk back toward the family room with my hair in my face. I enter the family room threshold and stand still, hands clenched, waiting for him to acknowledge me as a tingling feeling enters the edges of my scrunched knuckles. He gets up from the red velvet chair while snapping his fingers and screaming at the television. "Come on! Come On! Go! Go!" he hollers, as he turns to sit back down on the edge of the chair, he looks over at me and shouts,

"Bring me some Tabasco sauce!"

I turn and walk back through the dining room and into the kitchen, like the trained dog he says I am. I walk over to the refrigerator like a robot and pull open the ugly brown door. I look straight into the fridge and on the door—no Tabasco sauce. I begin to feel troubled and anxious again, and I start to panic. *Where is it, oh God help me, where is it?* I ask myself.

Searching and searching through the refrigerator, I rummage around each shelf, looking at each item one by one. I pick up each thing looking at it as I search. The anxiety in my stomach is really turning and twisting inside me now. He yells again, "What the fuck is taking so long?"

I jump and feel my brain wanting to take flight to the ceiling again. The atmosphere begins to feel strange, and then I realize there's no Tabasco sauce, and now I'm going to get into trouble. Shaking my hands up and down I start to whine.

"Oh God what do I do? How do I tell him? Oh God help me?"

I walk back into the family room, this time on the other side of the kitchen and through the bathroom, entering the family room.

"There's no Tabasco sauce," I stutter as I hold my hands together while pinching my skin so I won't float away and I'll concentrate.

He looks at me with the temper of a lion, his face, and neck is red, and purple veins are popping from his forehead. If I hadn't known any better, I would swear there's smoke emanating from his ears.

"What the fuck is wrong with you? You are one dumb mother fucker, you stupid fucking cunt."

He stands up from the chair and begins to come towards me; I back up into the wall while staring at his dark piercing eyes. Before I can catch my breath he grabs me by the back of my hair and lifts me off the floor. He heads me back through the bathroom and into the kitchen, in front of the refrigerator. He opens the ugly door on the refrigerator, while screaming as loud as he can with his vile words into my ear. His saliva lands on my face and hair as he yells.

"I have never seen anyone more fucking stupid than you; you are one dumb ass mother fucker, aren't you? A dumb fucking stupid mother fucker," he yells over and over, as he shakes my head up and down by the back of my hair.

He throws my small body into the metal shelves.

"UGH, oh God," I whisper, as I put my small hands up in front of me to protect myself from the blow. My head hits many bottles as he bashes me in and out of the cold fridge, my chest and thighs throb from the impact of being slammed into the metal bars. I feel the burning sensation of scratches on my chest and thighs from the sharp edges of the metal racks.

"Please, oh God, please stop, Daddy, please I'll make the eggs better. I'll find the Tabasco sauce, please Daddy, stop it," I cry and plead while extending my arms out as if to stop him.

"You fucking stupid whore," he yells, while keeping a strong grip on the back of my long curly hair. He springs me back out of the fridge and throws me back in again.

"Ugh," I hit the walls of the fridge.

"You stupid!"

"Ugh!"

"Fucking bitch!"

Everything that was in the refrigerator is now all over the kitchen floor. Stepping on lunch meat and bottles, he grabs more hair from the back of my head and gathers a tighter grip on me, all the while pushing my body further into the fridge, smashing the metal bars down toward the drawers as I cry and scream.

"Please stop I'll find it, I'll find it."

I'm wishing something—anything—will end this nightmare. Still keeping his iron-clad grip on the back of my hair, he pulls me out of the fridge again, only to push my head down towards the floor and walk me around the kitchen in circles while telling me how much of a dog I am, circling and circling the kitchen floor. With the force of his strong grip on the back of my head, I feel my long curly hair intertwine within his thick fingers, while my neck feels as though it is on fire from being bent down. I can't even put into words my feelings. I just wish for the horror to end. My father then swings me back towards the refrigerator.

"Ouch," I yelp, as I hit the inside door of the refrigerator and fall to the floor.

I scoot myself up against the wall next to the refrigerator and watch him pick up a bottle from the floor, one of the bottles that fell from the fridge. He comes over and grabs my hair from the side and with an even tighter hold he pulls back on my head, bending my neck.

"What the fuck does this say bitch?"

I can't speak; I can't even look at the bottle, even though it is in right in front of me. I can read the bottle, but it's as if it isn't even here. My body's frozen with fear. I feel numb, limp, and shaky. Everything is silent, almost muffled, but I can still hear him screaming obscenities at me, or I think I hear him. I see his lips moving. I feel my brain float toward the ceiling, and from there I watch myself scrunch up against the mint green fruit wallpaper on the wall. I no longer feel the pain in my body, as my eyes focus up at me and I'm now feeling myself floating against the ceiling. I see him standing over me, I see his dark hair and my tiny arms wrapped around my legs that are pressed into my chest.

Then, without warning, the silence is shattered and he shoves the Tabasco sauce bottle into my face, pushing it up against my cheek.

"You are one dumb stupid fucking piece of shit. Get the fuck out of my sight. I don't want to see your fucking face again for the rest of the fucking day, you fucking dog," he spits.

Still keeping his grip on my hair, he pushes me toward the bathroom. I try to scuttle away, but he reaches down and grabs my hair again, dragging me through the bathroom to the stairs that lead to the bedrooms. Pushing me by the back of my head we proceed up the curved staircase all the while keeping my hands in tight fists at my side. At the top of the stairs, we enter the threshold of my bedroom.

With a strong thrust, he pushes me toward the floor of the bedroom. I land on the hard floor, with my tiny hands catching my fall. He screams a few more nasty names at me, but I can't hear him anymore. My ears are ringing, my head feels like it weighs 1000 pounds, and my hair is stuck to my face from my tears and snot. He slams the door shut and locks it from outside with the hook-latch he installed some time before.

I stay in my room the rest of the day and throughout the night. I search for answers as to what just happened to me, but there is none. I've seen my father beat Barbra into the refrigerator many times before, and walk her around the kitchen floor in circles holding her by the back of the hair, too.

I crawl over to my bed and scoot my weak body up on the mattress and plop my head down on my pillow while I cup my hands around my ringing ears. My mind begins to wander. I hate myself and my life. I really hate being a dog. I feel so much inner pain and sadness from being a dog. *I wish I could be like other little girls, they aren't dogs.* Most of all, I feel shame in myself for making my daddy angry. *If only I saw the Tabasco sauce this wouldn't have happened*, I think, as if I somehow deserved what had just happened to me. Then I became angry with my mother for not being home, not that my mother would have stopped him. She never stops my father from hurting us, and when he gets really out of control, she just removes herself hysterically by running out of the house.

Then I became angry with Barbra. *If she had been here, then she could have cooked the eggs and they wouldn't have ended up lumpy. She would have found the Tabasco sauce. Then, none of this would have happened.*

Then I became angry at Marcia and how she hardly did anything with the toast part of the meal and then she got to go back outside and play while I got beat. *I hate her! She could have helped me more! I hate them! I hate them all!*

I go over to the window and look out at the cars driving on the interstate, thinking that this is everyone's fault. This was God's fault. God put me here with these people and made me live in this crazy place. Then I went back over to my bed and fell into it.

Lying there for what seemed like hours, I begin to feel guilty, as if I caused the abuse. I feel guilty for feeling hatred toward everyone. But I don't care, I still hate them.

Maybe if I'm better at being good, then that would make Daddy happy. If I can make Daddy happy, then I won't get beat or yelled at. I'm going to give this a try; I'm going to be the best little girl ever and everything will be better tomorrow.

Of course, at the age of ten my idea of being the best little girl ever didn't work. It wouldn't be the last time my face and body would see the inside of a refrigerator. Nor would it be the last time I was called a dog and circled around the kitchen floor. I would spend many years of my life always blaming myself for the horrific actions of my abusers. My way of making sense was thinking I deserved the abuse, because after all, I began believing I really was a dog like my father always told me.

* * *

A Healing Story...

"Fists of Pain" 2005

The exercise of putting my imaginary father in a chair and telling him how I really felt allowed me to gain feelings of power and control in overcoming the obstacles my father laid in my path as a child. For the first time I expressed my true feelings of anger, sadness and disgust of how I was treated. For the first time, I allowed myself to hear my own voice and hear my own liberties as a human being on this earth.

For the first time I knew what it feels like to have control over my own life and my own destiny. However, I didn't feel as though I was finished expressing my rage. I wanted to let it all out; I wanted to scream from the roof tops of every home. I hated my father for what he had done to me, how he treated me and I needed to feel empty of the rage that lay hidden inside me for so many years.

As I left my therapist's office and felt the rage linger inside my body, I felt my PTSD firing missiles from my brain to my body with a vengeance. The memories came at me like a slide show, flickering in front of my eyes as if I was under imagery interrogation.

Driving home I immediately locked my hands into iron-tight grips upon the steering wheel. I felt mad as hell and felt the need to explode this blood-boiling storm that's resonating within me.

I enter my driveway, throwing my car into park. I kick the car door open as I swing myself out as if I'm headed to a fire. Upon opening the garage door, I reach down and grab a 4'x4' canvas that's leaning against one of the concrete walls.

Covering my clothes with a painter's apron, I throw my handled basket of paints and metal painter's palate on top of Steve's long workbench. I squirt out different colors of paint. Purples, blues, yellows, green and red, all the colors of bruises; all colors of the marks my tiny body was tainted with.

With my palate full of blobs of deep colors I punch my fist into each color and then punch the canvas. I punch over and over until my fist begins to ache. Then I punch the canvas with the side of my fists, and then I punch the canvas with my other fist until that, too, begins to ache. I punch and punch with both fists until I begin to sob. Crying hysterically from the pain, the anger, and the shame.

All the anger that lay deep within is now turning into this great state of sorrow. The sadness is overwhelming and quite miserable. Releasing the rage opens up the emotion of grief within me, and now I feel the time has come to honor that little girl's feelings inside me.

I feel the pain in my abdomen, my sides, and in my back and chest. The pain was real when I was a child, and now as the adult I feel as though I'm shedding tears of pain that contaminated the essence of me.

I'm exhausted and physically wiped out. I'm tired and weary from the pollution of hurt I've vomited out of me onto the canvas. My painting now holds the pains of my emotions. The contusions that once were within my soul are slowly healing into scars.

Using art as a form of healing leaves me with the sense and belief that to deny a memory is to discard the past, to discard the human experience, to dispose of the event as if it were some object of no use. Therefore, I embrace my past with full knowledge of the pain it brings me because I know and feel that after the pain of healing, I will breathe a satisfaction of richness within my physical, emotional, spiritual, and psychological self.

"Fists of Pain" is my past and my present.

Chapter 6

The Electric Cord

The Trigger – 2005

Driving over the Mississippi River, the sign reads, "Welcome to Illinois." Only 120 more miles left to drive.
"Thank God," I say to myself as I toss and turn in my dream. I feel as though I'm being chased and I need to drive a little faster. The sun's going down and I feel a bit anxious. I hate driving in the dark.
A newer looking white car passes by me as I speed a little faster.
Looking down at the speedometer, it reads 72. I'm not going fast enough. If I don't hurry, he'll catch me. I need to go faster.
My mind slows down and I search inside the console for some music. I pull out CD after CD but I can't make out the labels; they're all fuzzy. I feel myself squinting my eyes to read, but there's no use, the fuzzy labels are unreadable. I pull out an Elton John CD, and pop it into the CD player. The first

song is "Saturday Night's Alright for Fighting." I begin to sing along as I pull my blanket closer to my neck and cuddle my hands together.

"My old man's drunker than a barrel full of monkeys and my old lady she don't care. My sister looks cute in her braces and boots, a handful of grease in her hair, la, la, la," I sing along.

I listen to the song and it reminds me of Barbra. The songs of the past only bring out the bad memories into the present. Right now my present is in a warm bed, even though this dream is taking me driving on a long, dark, paved road. I think about my sisters and feel the tears well up in my eyes.

Tears are streaming down my face as I snuffle into my pillow, while in my dream I stare at the red gleaming lights on the white car that passed me only a few moments ago.

All the sudden I get a jolt of awareness as the engine warning sounds – bling! bling! The engine light begins to flash.

"Damn-it!" I say out loud as I see myself pull the car over to the side of the road. I begin to panic again, overwhelmed by the urgency of the situation. Where are my Pepto-Bismol tablets?

I get out of the car, pull open the hood and look inside the engine area. I notice a loose cord; I fiddle with it by shaking it a bit, then slam the hood shut.

I look down at my watch as I get back in the car.

Putting the car back into "drive," I rush back onto the road. Only 50 miles to go. Please God; just give me 50 more miles, that's is all I need.

Looking at the red brake lights on the white car, I begin to think about the electrical outlets during my childhood. I remember how my mother wouldn't allow my sisters or me to leave the house unless we unplugged all the electrical cords from their outlets.

I thrash with intense fear. I'm being chased again. I'm still angry about the sleep deprivation we went through because of lectures about how not pulling the electrical cords from the outlet would lead to fires. In my dream I am a teenager. It's the middle of the night and I am sitting while my mother lectures me on the safety of electricity.

The dream focuses back to the fast moving white car, now in front of me. I am mesmerized by the events of the past. All of a sudden, an image of the loose cord from the engine area in the car flashes in my mind. A sharp jolt of lightning enters my body as my brain begins firing a non-stop movie clip, recalling the horrid event that left my sister Barbra black and blue, and Marcia and me scared out of our minds. I drive up to pass the little white car, and when I turn to see the driver, I gasp. It's me.

A flash of light enters my dream and I begin to breathe heavily and sweat profusely. This flashback terrifies me; it attacks my dream and turns it into a nightmare.

* * *

The Memory...

"OK kids, listen up! Your mother and I are going out tonight. I expect you girls to be good for your sister," Dad says as he and Mom leave the house, slamming the heavy oak door shut.

"Yippee! They left! We have the whole house to ourselves," I scream, dancing around in circles.

"Stop screaming you little brat," Barbra yells, looking at Marcia, who is bunched up into a ball on the couch, knees up to her chin, arms crossed over her legs.

I calm myself by taking deep breaths; I am so happy at not having my parents home. Mom and Dad never go out together and I like the idea of them leaving the three of us alone.

My favorite movie, Elvis Presley's "Girls! Girls! Girls!" is on tonight and I can't wait. I love Elvis Presley; he's my favorite actor. I love pretending I'm one of the Hawaiian girls, as I dance all over the hardwood floors of the living room. Dancing away, Marcia gets up and joins me.

"Knock it off you brats," Barbra barks. "I have something I need to talk to you about."

I keep twirling around in circles. "So talk, and if you're gonna to be mean we ain't gonna listen to you, right Marcia?"

Marcia nods in agreement as if to say, "Yeah, what she said."

Barbra stands up from the couch, adjusting her bell-bottom jeans with tattered hems.

"Look, I'll give you guys fifty cents each to go to the pool tomorrow, but only if you'll keep a secret."

Marcia and I quit and stare at Barbra. It must be serious if she's offering us money.

"A secret? I love secrets, what is it. What is it?" Marcia asks, jumping up and down with excitement.

"Ok, here's the program, now listen up," Barbra demands.

Marcia and I tuck our hair over our ears, while we lick our lips and clinch our fingers together.

"I have a friend coming over."

"When?" Marcia interrupts.

"Now," Barbra says. "His name is Doug, and I want you guys to be nice. I'll let you guys watch T.V. in Mom and Dad's room, okay?"

I look at Marcia. She's scared, and I am, too.

"What's wrong?" Barbra asks.

"What if we get caught?" I ask.

"Look, you're not going to get caught. Mom and Dad are out, and Doug is only stopping by. He isn't going to stay long. You guys can sit on the floor in their room, so they won't know you were in there, okay?"

"Alright." Marcia and I answer in unison. We shrug our shoulders, as if to say, whatever you say.

"I hear Doug knocking. He's here! He's here!" I scream, my eyes widen and I jump up and down, almost losing my clumsy brown clogs.

"Shut-up, now go upstairs," Barbra hisses.

Marcia and I run behind the red velvet chair and huddle together as if we're miniature football players. Glaring out one side of the chair while Marcia glares out the other side, we watch as the curly blond-haired teenager enters our house. I'm excited but scared; a boy has never come into our house before, and Barbra only has one girlfriend that we know about.

"Pssst," Marcia whispers, poking my arm, "he has pimples like Barbra."

"Yep, sure does. I wonder if he squeezes them like she does."

"I dunno."

We stay behind the chair and watch as they sit on the Mexican-style sofa. Marcia and I giggle at them.

Just then, my father flies through the front door, banging the heavy door against the wall as he enters in a rage. His face is as deep red as fire, and his temper is fuming with evil. I swear his eyes are all dark, without any white in them at all, as if he is some kind of demon.

"I caught cha, you little whore!"

Barbra and Doug jump up and run toward the kitchen. Marcia and I freeze and then grab each other. I squeeze my hands into fists and squish my eyes shut and pray. Please God, please make it stop, please! I can feel Marcia's body shake.

Marcia begins to make sounds like a muffled puppy; I open my eyes and see my father. He grabs Barbra by the back of her hair with a stretched reach of his arm as she attempts to run toward the kitchen. Doug runs out of the living room through the dining room. Then the red velvet chair Marcia and I are squatting behind smashes up against the wall as Barbra is thrown into it.

Marcia takes off running one way toward the curved staircase as I take off running the other way toward the dining room. I run through the dining room and into the kitchen. My plan is to run around to the other side of the kitchen, through the bathroom that leads to the curved staircase.

But my plan comes to a screeching halt when I run into the kitchen. There stands Doug, and my mother is blocking the back door preventing him from leaving. I'm in shock!

This is the first time I see my mother be a part of my father's sick games. My father pushes me out of the way as he pounds into the kitchen, screaming. His face is still beet red and purple; the veins are popping out of his forehead; curse words fall out of his mouth like hot lava.

"If I ever see your fucking ass around this house again I will beat the shit out of you and your parents. Now get the fuck out!" He yells as he pokes the kid in the chest with his index finger.

Doug doesn't say anything. He's clearly traumatized, and I can tell by the gigantic size of his eyes that he's really scared. His face is as red as a ruby and he's shaking, holding up his hands in front of his face as though my father is going to punch him.

My mother stands holding the door open for Doug to go out and looks down at me as if to say, "This is your entire fault. You rotten kids made him mad, now look what you've done!"

I can hear Barbra crying and moaning in the living room. I run back into the dining room to peek around the cased opening into the living room. I want to see how bad he hurt her. Her red hair is stuck to her face and she's shaking like a leaf. She is on the floor, leaning against the red chair. She looks up at me, and then buries her head in the seat cushion. My hands still in tight fists, I make a brave attempt to whisper to her.

"Pssst, Barbra, you ok?"

Right then, I sense my father standing next to me. He starts screaming at her again, calling her bad names. He stomps over to her and slaps her really hard in the head, over and over again. She gets up from the chair and tries to run, screaming and squealing, but he has a hand full of her hair. He tugs and throws her body through the air. She lands against the wall above the couch, and then falls against the side of the sofa.

I'm frozen in fear. I just stand there watching him beat her and beat her. Then he rips the electrical cord out from the television and begins to whip her with the cord, hitting her on her back and head. I can't help but wince. She's screaming so loud, pleading for him to stop, but he won't. He keeps hitting her over and over with the cord. I can hear whips piercing her skin with every blow he lands. She begins to drop toward the floor with her hands skimming the paneled walls.

I close my eyes and pray really hard, squishing my eyes shut, but her screams keep me from concentrating as I cry in terror. The louder she screams, the more jumpy I get. I get so scared that I pee in my pants right there on the dining room floor. Then I jump from being startled at my mother's voice.

"Get up to your room."

Bawling with fear, I sprint to the stairs, running right into my bedroom. I slam the door behind me and look around the room for Marcia. I shake my hands up and down and bust out wimps of sound as I search frantically for Marcia. My hair whips around and sticks to my tears and snot as I check under the beds. I call her name and find her in the back corner of her closet, scrunched into a ball, sobbing, rocking back and forth. I shut the closet door behind me and run over to her, where I scrunch up into a ball next to her. We both weep and my hands throb in pain.

I look down and see blood on my hands. I squeezed my hands so hard into fists that I broke the skin with my fingernails. The sight of the blood on my hands makes me shake. I pray and pray for the nightmare to end and I can sense Marcia praying, too. Please make it stop; please make it go away. I want it to go away, please make the screams and yelling stop.

Barbra's punishment comes to an end when my father gets tired and worn out from the physical exertion of beating her. He opens the front door to leave, but not before yelling at my mother.

"See, do you fucking see? This is why we can't make it work, because it's that fucking reason right there!"

Marcia and I hear his words and look at each other with surprise, as this is the first we learn that my parents are thinking of separating.

Marcia and I are lucky, but not Barbra, she complains her ribs hurt from the beating, but she can't tell. We can never tell. Really bad things will happen to us if we tell. We must always protect the family secret, even though we don't know we're really keeping a secret.

Soon after that incident my parents did separate and then divorced and my mother moved us away to an apartment. Although she never really stopped seeing my father, and we did have our visitations with him, life was not as bad. Well, not until years later.

*   *   *

The Healing — 2005

The phone rings.

"When are you coming?" Marcia asks.

"I'm leaving now, I'll call you when I get there," I say as I throw a few clothes into my almost-packed black duffel bag.

"Are you sure you want to go there? Are you sure you want to do this?"

"Yes, I'm sure. Why? Are you scared?"

"Well, kind of, I mean, I don't know. I'm sure it will be fine."

"Are you worried?"

"No, I'll be fine, but what about Barbra?"

"What about her?" I ask.

"Shouldn't she be part of this?"

"She will be part of this. We will make this about her too," I say. "You know we have our differences; things have to get worked out between us. Besides, I haven't spoken to Barbra in almost three years. Don't worry, we will do this for her too, and you can explain it to her." I say, trying to hurry the conversation to a close.

"Yeah, I think you're right. She's been in therapy now for awhile and it's really helping her. I just wish --."

"Marcia, I love Barbra, and even though our differences have set us apart, we will connect back together when the time is right for both of us."

"I know, it's very hard, sometimes sad, I just wish things were different. We could all get along and heal from this." Marcia says.

"Marcia, our relationship has blossomed since that time I came to you and asked you about writing the book. My relationship with Barbra will heal, too. We just need to approach it when the time is right for both of us."

"I know, I mean I guess this is all part of the process," she says. "Anyway, drive safely."

"I will. I'm getting Scott and Stephen in the car now and I'll call you when I get to Sean's apartment."

During the seven-hour drive back to Omaha, Scott and Stephen play video games while discussing how they're going to manipulate their older brother into paint balling and buying them another video game.

I think about my conversation with Marcia and how I also wish things could be different for Barbra and me. I wish Barbra could see her pain the way I see her pain, and how it has taken over her life. I wish I could be driving back home for a pleasant visit with my family. But our lives are different; we are and will always be struggling with the effects of our abusive childhoods. We can't change that, no one can, but that doesn't mean we can't heal from it, and that is what keeps me going.

I know Barbra and I will find our way back to each other, just as Marcia and I have. It's only a matter of time, and a lot of healing.

Pulling into my son Sean's apartment complex, I feel relieved and tired. The time is already past 9:00 p.m. and Scott and Stephen are wide-awake. They're eager to see their big brother and take over his new PlayStation.

It takes us about fifteen minutes to clear out the car and make our way into Sean's apartment. I drop the bags in his living room, while reaching up to give my son a kiss and ask to use the phone. I call Marcia.

"I made it here, can you meet me here around 9 or 10 in the morning?"

"Oh yes, I'll be there early, I can't wait to see you."

"I can't wait to see you, either, and don't forget, we'll need a shovel."

"Ok, no problem, I'll bring the shovel," Marcia says, "See ya in the morning, love you."

"I love you, too."

"Mom," Sean asks, "What are you going to do with a shovel?"

"Sean, I know your career of choice is enforcing the law, but sometimes I think you watch way too many cop shows."

"Ok," he said, "I'm just not so sure about you two and a shovel."

The next morning Marcia shows up with her youngest son, David, who will spend the morning playing video games with Scott and Stephen. While the kids begin showing each other their games, Sean informs me he's planning on taking the kids swimming while Marcia and I go out for the day. Marcia and I give the kids kisses as we head out the door, shovel in hand.

"Are you sure this is going to work?" Marcia asks.

"I don't know, you brought a pretty puny shovel here," I say while getting into the car.

"You think it's too small?"

"I'm not so sure about the shoveling capacity of this shovel, but I have a gut feeling we need to put this to rest." I say as we drive toward our old house.

"It's going to be so weird setting foot on that place," Marcia says while looking out the window.

"Yeah I know. It's going to feel really strange."

Marcia and I take a few deep breaths as we pull the car up to the curb in front of the now empty lot of where we grew up. We both sit in silence and look out the car window, imagining the house, our lives and the nightmares that once lurked on that property.

"Do you know when the house burned down?"

"It looks so small," Marcia whispers, "Can't remember, it burned down a long time ago, electrical fire, I read."

"Hmmm, that's weird, all those lectures mom gave us about electrical fires and leaving the plugs in the walls, and the house that held the nightmares burns down by electrical fire."

"That is weird, isn't it?" Marcia asks.

"You're right, it looks really small, too small."

"Now what?" Marcia asks.

"We get out the paper and write all the lies they told us, then we take this red pen and write 'LIE' across their words."

Taking out our pads of paper, Marcia searches for her blue pen. I grab mine and start writing the lies out in huge letters, one per piece of paper.

"Slut –LIE."

"Stupid cock sucker son of a bitch- LIE."
"No good piece of shit – LIE."
"YOU'RE A DOG-LIE,"
"YOU'RE A DOG –LIE"
"YOU'RE A DOG-LIE, LIE, LIE, LIE, LIE, LIE, LIE."
"Cunt –LIE."
"Ugly Bitch – LIE."
"Whore – LIE."
"Fucking cock sucker- LIE."
"Brainless bitch – LIE."

Marcia watches as I rip sheet after sheet of the lies our parents told us, and decides she can write in small letters and use one sheet of paper. When we're both satisfied, I gather the sheets of paper and head out of the car toward the trunk.

Marcia slams her door shut while I grab the puny green shovel and shut the trunk. We walk around the lot, which is full of tall weeds and grasshoppers.

"Where do you want to bury the lies?" Marcia asks.

"Ahhhh...well...I'm not sure, this lot looks so small now."

"I know. How about in the back of the lot under the big oak tree, were we used to have the tire swing?" Marcia suggests this as she marches through the tall skinny weeds.

"Good place."

Marcia and I begin to dig a hole next to the oak tree, and as we're digging we both begin to think back to when we were kids, playing on that tire swing. We reminisce about the fun times we had swinging.

"Throw the lies in the hole," I whisper, satisfied with the work we've done.

"How could they call us names like that?" Marcia asks, kneeling down placing her paper in the hole.

"We were just little kids," she says. "We didn't deserve that."

I kneel down next to her, placing my hand on the back of her shoulder.

"No child deserves to be treated that way." I say as I lean into the hole and grab a handful of dirt to throw on top of the sheets of paper.

Marcia and I scoop up dirt with our bare hands and throw it into the hole. Silence takes over as if we are at a funeral grieving for the lies.

Standing, staring at the grave of lies, I have one hand on the shovel as I lean to see the size of the lot. I want to figure out where the clothesline once stood. Marcia stares at the ground at her feet and then begins to walk around as if she's searching for something.

"Do you remember where the clothesline was?" I ask.

"This lot seems so skinny and narrow," I say as I brush my hair from my face.

Marcia walks toward the edge of the lot, where the sidewalk used to be, and I watch the cars pass by. Leaning on the too-small green shovel, I stare at the openness of the lot. I glance back over to where I think the clothesline once stood, all the while imagining myself being tied up. Out of nowhere a horn blasts, waking me out of my trance. I jump and look back toward the passing cars. They honk now, but never when I was tied up to that clothesline, I think as a tear enters my eye.

"What are you looking for?" I yell as Marcia makes her way to the other end of the weedy lot, still looking down, searching.

"I'm trying to find the path of rocks," she says without looking up.

"The rocks from the gravel drive and the ones that were spread out along the sidewalk from where he kept his used cars for sale?" I ask as I walk over to her.

"Yes, where are the rocks?"

"Do you think when the house burned down someone came and took the rocks?" she asks.

"Probably not, they're just concrete rocks, the kind you drive on. Why would someone want those ugly rocks?" I ask as I help her search.

"Where are they?" Marcia presses.

"Why are the rocks so important?"

"They're not, I just want to see them. Don't you remember how they would make us bring in the rocks to kneel on in the corner of the dining room?"

"Ugh, I hated that."

"Let's look through the weeds," I say. "Maybe they're here in the weeds, even though it has been almost 30 years."

Marcia and I begin pulling the weeds, making a clearing in the ground, and as we do we see the ugly concrete rocks poking up through the dry brown dirt.

"Use the shovel," Marcia says excitedly, "maybe we can dig them up."

"This sad shovel of yours is going to be broken by the time you get it home," I say. "We've already put a bad bend in it from digging the 'lie' grave." I force the shovel into the hard dirt.

Marcia and I dig up rock after ugly rock, awful things that were once used as our punishment.

"Where are you going?" Marcia asks as she watches me get up and head toward the car.

"I'm going to get a lunch pail from the trunk so we have somewhere to put the rocks."

"What will we do with them?" Marcia asks as she stands up, brushing her khaki short overalls with her small, manicured hands.

"We can divide them up into thirds and get matching bowls," I say, "One for you, one for me, and one for Barbra."

"That's a great idea," Marcia says. "You know with all these cars honking at us, you would think someone could have stopped when we were running for our lives in the middle of the night."

"You would think," I say, "but that was a different time. People had a way of turning a blind eye." I bend down and throw the rocks into the red lunch pail.

"Sad," she says, "very sad."

"Hey, did you guys lose something?" I look up to see that a brown-haired boy who looks to be about thirteen is watching us.

"Umm, I guess we did," I sputter as I look up toward the teen boy standing on his skateboard.

"Whatcha lose?"

"I s'pose we lost our childhoods and we've come back to claim them." I explain as I dig into the dirt, searching for more rocks.

"Ahhh, okay, want some help?"

"No thanks, I think we've got it covered, thank you anyway," Marcia says as she throws a handful of rocks into the lunch pail.

I pick up the lunch pail, which now has at least 75 concrete rocks, and place it in the trunk of the car. I look at Marcia and ask if she's ready to go or if she wants to stay a little longer. She's ready. The lies are now buried at the base of the oak tree. We both say our good-byes as we stand by the car, looking at the lot one last time. Without saying a word I take a deep breath and feel a great sense of relief come over me. I open up the back car door.

"Ok kids, get in, we're getting out of this retched place."

Marcia looks at me as if I've just gone mad.

"What do you mean?" she asks.

"I mean, I'm taking all the kids out of this horrid place. They don't belong here anymore. This is their past, and now we're taking them to the future. Do you understand?" I ask.

"I think so."

"We are taking the little girls we once were out of here," I say. "We're taking the little girls inside of us out of here and into a safe place, we're taking them home."

"Wow, we're finally leaving this place; we're free, we're free to be safe now," she says, her voice cracking with excitement as she places her hands on her face as if to comfort herself.

I slam the back door shut and we get in. When we pull away, neither one of us looks back.

Marcia and I find three matching bowls to house the ugly rocks, and as we do we find bags of pretty rocks to intermix with them.

Marcia and I decide the pretty rocks represent our lives and our healing and the ugly rocks represent our past and what we've come from. Together, we make our bowls of rocks and realize there is something missing.

"We need to place something inside these bowls to represent us, don't you think?" I ask.

"What about three candles, one for each of us?"

"This is what healing is all about, Marcia, great idea."

Marcia and I place the three candleholders in the center of the bowls and decide that the candles must always touch. There is power in numbers, and as long as the three candles remain together, they will always be able to support each other to stay lit.

A few months after Marcia and I buried the lies, Barbra and I began talking, and now all three of us together are healing the pains of our past.

Chapter 7

Grandma

The Trigger...

The year is 2001 and I'm traveling through the streets of Jerusalem, Israel. I find myself walking up a winding cobble stone path, taking in the sweet smell of the air and the warm sun. I notice a sign that reads "Yad Vashem," the Holocaust Memorial Museum. Entering the museum, I am overwhelmed by its massive size; the museum is divided up into sections and has outer courts.

I start my journey learning about the museum by walking along a path of newly planted trees with signs depicting different countries and the number of people who perished from each of those countries. I glance upon a sign that reads *Romania*. Continuing with my walk I read a sign that says *Russia*. My mother's family is from both Russia and Romania. Though I have a connection to this place, and the people, I am still a very disconnected person.

The years of abuse have left me with the sensation my brain is a fuzzy ball of yarn along with a constant feeling of numbness. I look at the signs from Russia and Romania and long for a sense of connection to my ancestors. I try to imagine what life was like for my relatives during the time of the Holocaust, but I can't. My brain does not function in the capacity for which I desire and my emotions are not responding to my requests. Something is blocking me from connecting. I feel as though my skin is thick and hard, and nothing can penetrate it, much like the skin of an elephant. I wear this hard, thick skin with great sadness because I do not possess the ability to connect, even when I consciously try.

Walking through the main building of the museum, I see large photos depicting mass graves, Jews being tortured by Nazis, and the ghettos Jews were forced to live in. Still, I am not able to connect; I'm not able to feel the pain and the cries shown in these horrific pictures. I try so hard to concentrate as I walk through the halls of this museum looking at the monstrous pictures one by one. Yet, I'm unable to feel the sadness, the heartache of why this museum was built. How am I supposed to "never forget" if I can't feel?

I find myself right in the middle of the children's museum, another division of Yad Vashem. People are lining up to view an exhibit I hadn't noticed before. I decide to follow the crowd and get in line. The line starts to move, but I don't know what the line is for or where it goes.

The line of people moves slowly and I find myself enclosed in a narrow room with glass walls on my left and my right. I'm very curious as to where I am, so I asked a broad-shouldered, elderly woman wearing a big furry hat and a plush brown coat who was standing in front of me.

"What is this place?"

She turns toward me with tears in her eyes, wiping them away with her black cotton glove. She responds in a rough, low European accent. "We are experiencing what the children experienced as they walked to their deaths."

She pulls a Kleenex from her huge purse, dabs her eyes, and blows her nose. She shakes her head and looks at me and my emotionless expression with a puzzled look. In shock, I feel an emotion well up inside of me. I feel shame in myself for not connecting. I can see in her face and sense in her look that she has sympathy for me.

The line continues to move forward, and as I move along I hold my head low, feeling shame and sorrow. Suddenly, I hear a burst of cries come from the front of the line. I jump at the sound and crane my neck to see where the cries are coming from. I can't see who's making the noise, but when I stretch up onto my toes I notice the glass walls look smoky. The room becomes very narrow and the smoke gray color radiates the environment around me. I can't take my eyes off the smoky walls, and before I know it the walls feel as though they are closing in on me, and the narrow hall is filled with smoke. My mind starts shooting flashbacks through me like daggers attempting to pierce my elephant hide. The cries from people in front of me are getting louder and the people behind me are bursting out with heartfelt cries of sadness and horror.

I begin to feel scared and my mind starts to race. My hands are trembling, my body begins to shake, and my head feels warm and fuzzy. This flashback is very strong and I feel like my brain is aching with pressure. I can't suppress it. I'm trying to push it away like I have always done, but this time it's pounding and pounding inside my head as if I'm going to explode. Placing my hands on my head I begin to throttle my body back and forth while balancing on my heels.

I can hear my grandmother's voice; the sounds of cries from the people in the line become muffled as I hear my grandmother's words in my ears. I want to run and hide, but there is nowhere to go. The smoke-filled walls are on both sides of me, and the crying people are in front of and behind me. The only thing I can hear are the horrific words being spoken to me in my grandmother's voice from my own flashback.

I feel as if I'm bouncing off the glass walls. Turning in circles, I try to find a way out. Her words are getting louder and stronger. I feel frightened at knowing I'm hearing my father's mother speaking into my head. I squish my eyes shut and cover my ears with the palms of my hands. Stop. Go away. I can't take this. Stop. Stop. Stop it.

This audio flashback burns inside my head as her voice hammers at my psyche. I've had many audio flashes of my name being called but never have I had an audio flashback as painful as this.

I can feel my eyes fill up with tears. My throat swells with sadness as I sense the pain and anguish of the children who walked to their deaths. I cry and sob all though the rest of the narrow, smoke-filled hall. For the first time, I've connected with the Jews who perished, the Jews who suffered through the hands of evil.

I run out of the museum into the sunshine, wiping my nose with my sleeve and my eyes with my fingers. Shaking like a leaf, I remember the pictures. The monstrous pictures I walked past but could not mentally connect with. I run back to the main part of the museum. I so badly want to connect with the sad, hurt people in the pictures. I race through the museum as people stare at me like I'm some kind of crazy woman. I don't care; I rush as I need to see the picture that is forever stuck in my mind, the picture of the beautiful woman holding her baby to her chest, running from a Nazi who is pointing his pistol at her back.

Frantically running through the aisles of pictures, I finally find her. I stand there staring at her, the fear on her face, the tension in her body. I imagine what she must have felt, what she must have thought as she ran for her life and the life of her child. Tears run down my face as I stare at her and the horror of it all.

* * *

The Memory…

"Hurry the fuck up!" Dad bellows from the living room. "I don't have all fucking day to wait around for you. Ahhhh FUCK-ME!"

Moving as fast as we can, Marcia and I run in and out of the bathroom and our bedroom trying to get our teeth brushed and get dressed as fast as we can. We can't afford to draw attention to ourselves by falling over from the fear that has entered our bodies. We run around like little whirling tornadoes. Mom's in the living room sitting on the red and black Mexican floral couch, not saying a word as Dad screams and yells his obscenities at us.

Dad has decided to show up for his weekend to spend quality time with his children. My stomach is in knots, and my heart feels heavy. I also feel faint from the fear, but I know better than to speak and tell him I don't want to go spend the weekend with him. I feel as though I'm just put here in this world to be punished. I have no voice and no mind, and I've already begun to lose my soul. Soon I will be a lifeless human wandering throughout this world without connection. At twelve-years-old, the small hope of escaping the evil life I have with my parents will soon diminish.

Running down the steps as fast as we can without tumbling over head over heels, Marcia and I get into my father's run down, rusted out, shit-brown, two-door Duster. Marcia gets in front while I climb into the back.

Our drive is like any other ride with my father, chaotic and crazy. Weaving in and out of traffic like a NASCAR driver, he starts to scream, yell, and flip other drivers the bird. It doesn't matter who he yells at. It can be the McDonald's manager on his way to work or a woman driving her kids to school. He'll yell at all drivers; even those driving on the other side of town will all get his wrath.

"Get the fuck off the road, you whore!" Dad yells at an elderly woman who's driving slower than a turtle.

Without seatbelts and sliding on the cracked and torn vinyl seats, Marcia and I get tossed from side to side every time he turns the steering wheel. Then, as always, he turns his anger toward his children. In a loud, angry voice my father informs us that he's taking us to Grandma's house, his mother.

"I have things I have to get done and I can't have you two with me," he says.

Good, the asshole is going to leave us, I think to myself.

The tripled tarred streets in Grandma's trailer court are full of potholes. Dad drives through the potholes like he's driving a tank. Marcia and I get tossed from seat to ceiling with every one. We know better than to complain, so Marcia and I stay silent as our stomachs jump up and down.

Coming to an abrupt, screeching halt in front of Grandma's run down brown and white-colored trailer, Marcia and I get out of the car as quickly as we can move. Dad drives off in a hurry and takes a cloud of broken asphalt and smoke with him. Marcia and I look at each other and roll our eyes in embarrassment as we open the rickety metal gate that fences in the front part of Grandma's ten-foot patch of yard. Marcia and I walk up the wobbly three black metal steps that lead to the front door. We both lean over the rail and peer at her torn up garden with deformed carrots growing through the ground.

Grandma opens the door wide enough to nearly knock me and Marcia off the three-by-three platform attached to the black steps. Marcia and I take a step back as the cigarette smoke rolls out of the trailer.

"Where's your father?" Grandma asks with a cigarette hanging out of the left side of her mouth. Marcia and I walk into the stale-smelling trailer. "He dropped us off," we say, somberly.

Looking around the living room I take notice of the dried up dead plants and flourishing cactuses. There's a burning cigarette in the ashtray that's sitting on the coffee-stained, cigarette-burned sofa table. Marcia takes off running toward the back of the trailer and pulls out an old torn up toy box. Rummaging through the rusted-out trucks that have no tires, Marcia pulls out a broken-limbed Barbie. I maneuver my way through the living room and plop down on the bed/couch, which has a multi-colored crocheted afghan spread out on the flat mattress.

Grandma brings over a child-sized pea soup colored chair with rusted out metal legs and sits on it next to the sofa table. Sitting on the couch, I look at Grandma. Her pores are deep and her skin is heavily wrinkled. I ask if I can watch TV. Without hesitation, Grandma turns on the 10" black and white tube and asks if we want some of her homemade cookies. Of course Marcia and I love Grandma's cookies (that taste like cigarette smoke) and we dive right in.

Sports, and more sports. That's all that's on television, all three channels. I want to watch cartoons, but of course it's 1977 and anything on television after 12 noon on Saturday is sports. The educational channel comes in fuzzy, but I get off the bed/couch and turn the metal dial to channel twelve anyway.

"Leave it there!" Grandma yells as soon as the signal comes in. "I want you girls to watch this. You need to watch this."

I look at the television and see horrible pictures of skinny people with sunken faces.

"Why do I need to watch this?" I ask.

"You just do. Now don't give me any lip, just sit down and watch it," Grandma barks.

"What is it, what is it?" Marcia asks.

"It is a show about the Holocaust, now sit down and watch it," Grandma yells. Marcia sits next me with her legless Barbie cradled in her arms. *I don't understand what the heck this woman's problem is but she can be so nasty at times*, I think, looking at Grandma. Static channel or not, I want to watch the show because I've heard about the Holocaust in school.

The pictures that flash through the fuzzy screen are horrible to look at. Men are lying in bunk beds with their skin attached to their bones like a surgeon's rubber glove on a hand. Their shaved heads have sores and their mouths are dry and cracked. Women are being shoved into room-sized showers naked, but water doesn't come out of the showerheads. Instead they scream and drop dead.

Then pictures of the graves. Bodies upon bodies cover each other like human building blocks. Soon a little girl flashes on the screen she looks to be my age, around twelve sitting by herself, her head down, eating crackers. A Nazi walks past her. I can sense the fear in her. She flinches as he walks by, the same way I always flinch when Dad's around. Then before I know it, the Nazi turns around, walks past her again and shoots her. I can't believe it. I suddenly feel sick to my stomach. I can't breathe. I'm in shock.

Marcia's so busy playing with her legless Barbie that she doesn't even see the horror on the television. Looking over at my grandmother's dark circles under her eyes and with a sad, puzzled look on my face, I put my hands on my cheeks and say, "He just killed her. He just walked past and shot her. How could he do that? How could he? She's just a girl, like me."

"Well now, do you see how lucky you are?" Grandma asks sarcastically.

I swallow hard; I can't speak. I don't know what my grandmother wants me to say. I feel so confused and sad; I don't know why she thinks I'm lucky.

Marcia gets up from the couch, opens the front door and goes out with a large puff of smoke behind her. She's twirling her Barbie in circles by its chopped hair. Leaving the door open, Grandma gets up from the child-sized chair to shut the stained, hollow-core front door. Still puzzled, I look up at my grandmother's wrinkled face as she shuts the door behind Marcia while lighting another cigarette, even though one's burning in the ashtray next to me.

Grandma pulls the ugly green chair closer to me and sits in it while puffing non-stop on the long cigarette.

"You see, you're lucky because you have German blood," she says as she spits some tobacco from her lip.
"What?" I ask.
"Don't you understand?" she asks.
My mind is still thinking about the girl who was shot on the TV. With a scared feeling and not having a freaking clue as to what she is talking about, I begin to feel frantic.
"No, I don't understand," I said, terrified.
"Look, the Jewish people got what they deserved!" she blurts out angrily.
"Because your mother is a Jew, you are a Jew, but, you have German blood, too. You might have been saved, you see. You are lucky because you have German blood!" she says with an evil snicker.
Is she telling me I would have deserved to be murdered like the little girl in the movie because I'm a Jew? Or is she telling me, I should be lucky because I have German blood and might have been saved from the evil Nazis?
I look down at my small, frail hands and think about the girl who was shot by the Nazi. She didn't do anything, she was just sitting there eating her crackers, how could she have deserved that? My grandmother's words, "The Jewish people got what they deserved," shot through me like the bullet shot through the little girl on the T.V.
"Do you understand?" she asks.
I don't say anything. I feel hurt inside, and I want to run away, but I can't move. I look around the living room and notice all the pictures of my cousins—baby pictures, school pictures, and so on. Now I think I know why my grandmother doesn't have any pictures up of me and my sisters. My grandmother hates Jews and I'm a Jew. She hates me for being Jewish. But I don't even know what a Jew is. My mother doesn't tell us anything about being Jewish. The only thing I know is that she was raised Orthodox and her family is Jewish. How am I different because I'm Jewish? What does it mean?

I look back over at my grandmother, who's putting away the cookies.

"What about the babies, what did the babies do?" I ask, afraid now.

"What is wrong with you?" Grandma asks, clearly aggravated. "The babies would grow up and become bigger Jews!" she said, her anger affecting her voice.

I swallow hard and I feel flustered. My heart feels sad, empty. I feel completely ashamed of whom I am. I have a mother who was raised an orthodox Jew and a German father who was raised by a Nazi. What does that make me?

Marcia crashes through the front door, falling on her legless and now headless Barbie.

"Dad's coming! I can hear his horn!" she yells.

My father loves honking his car horn; he honks just for the sake of honking. Marcia throws the defunct Barbie into the tattered toy box and runs back out the door. I walk out of Grandma's trailer without saying a word, closing the door behind me.

I leave my grandmother's trailer feeling like a different person than when I entered. Why does she hate me? What have I done? I slowly walk to the car with my hair covering my face.

Between the abuse from my father and hate-filled words of my grandmother, I'm now well on my way to imprisoning myself from other humans. I was forever changed, and I hated them for that.

* * *

A Healing Story…

The year is now 2005 and I'm on a bus headed to Jerusalem from Tel-Aviv. I have come back to Israel to face the horrifying words my grandmother spoke to me 28 years ago, by going back to Yad VaShem.

Sitting on the bus, I remember the day I sat in my grandmother's living room and the words she said to me. I remember feeling as though I wanted to run away from that crazy family and all their misery. I remember looking at my hands as though they were filled with stained blood from the poison of her hatred toward me and all the other Jews of the world.

Then I remembered her death. It was two years ago when my sister Marcia called me and told me Grandma had died. She was 89-years-old, and I wondered if she had ever found some peace in her life. I wondered if she remembered the evil words she had spoken to me on that summer day in 1977. Then I remembered how I never went to her funeral, and how I wasn't ready to deal with the emotions of her death. But today I'm ready to deal with her death and the effects of her evil words, both contributing to my PTSD. I need to know if I will hear her voice when I enter the doors of the Holocaust museum like I did four years ago.

Opening the taxi door in front of Yad VaShem I get out and stand looking at the new addition since my last trip here. I worry at the reoccurrence of my PTSD, the audio flashback of my grandmother's voice. I pull my sunglasses off my face and look up toward the sky as if to ask God for strength and guidance as I walk toward the big glass entrance doors of the museum.

Once inside, I can feel my heart pounding as I walk through the main entrance and cross a bridge from the outside into a building made of Jerusalem stone. Inside the museum it is dark and the first thing I see is a crowd of people watching a film. I hurry around them and walk down a path that leads to many sections of open rooms. As I enter the first room I notice the walls are filled with photographs of children. The children pictured are smiling and playing with each other. The backgrounds are of war-torn buildings of the ghettos in which they lived. The sight of these children brings me to place my hand on my Silver Star of David that hangs from my neck. I then begin to connect myself with the pictures and the children's beautiful faces. Then I remember the famous picture of the woman running through the wheat field holding her baby to her chest while a Nazi holds up his pistol, ready to murder them. My eyes begin to tear up as I remember and I continue to walk through the sections of rooms.

Stepping into the third room, I begin to look more intensely at the photos of Nazis. Each photo I look at reminds me of the cold, hard, monstrous face of the Nazi in the T.V. program I watched all those years ago in my grandmother's trailer. I find myself racing through the photos as I feel myself becoming physically ill. My stomach is turning and I begin to feel as though I am going to puke right in the middle of the room. I begin to talk to myself and the words I choose to say startle me. *She didn't know what she was saying; she didn't know what she was saying.* I repeat this over and over as I walk from room to room. *This has nothing to do with Jews, Grandma; this has everything to do with hate, evil wickedness.* I tell myself these things as the tears begin to drip from my eyes. *She didn't know what she was saying.* In the last room I come upon another photo of children smiling; their faces bring relief to my essence. I take a step back to fully see all of their faces. I want to remember these children with their smiles. I step back and feel the level of the floor drop. I look down and notice that my feet are on a wide piece of glass with old tattered shoes in the bottom of the floor. I clench my shawl, my stomach turns in knots, and my head begins to spin.

I walk briskly out of the room and up the hall, where I see a balcony standing behind double glass doors; all the while tears are streaming down my sunburned cheeks. I open up the massive glass doors and see Jerusalem staring back at me. I stand in front of the steel bars of the balcony and take in deep breaths of the sweet air. I breathe for a few minutes and then realize my PTSD isn't shooting sounds or pictures through my head. I've either learned to control it or there's no reason for it to return. It's been a year or so since I've had a flashback. I feel the relief of not going through that pain and decide to press on toward the children's memorial section.

I find the children's section of the museum and take in a deep breath before entering. As I exhale I take hold of a steel rail that's connected to the wall. The room is very dark, and I stop to allow my eyes to adjust. The room is nearly pitch black and the only light is emanating from candles. The music is the gut-wrenching low sounds of moaning cellos. I take baby steps as I walk; toward my left are glass walls filled with thousands of lit candles scattered on black boxes from floor to ceiling. I make my way around the center glass wall and find a corner in which to stand. Standing in the corner of darkness, looking at all the candles flicker, the tears flow out of me. The tears of pure sadness overshadow my being. My gut is wrenching when I feel myself begin to double over in excruciating pain. The agony is overwhelming. The poor babies. Why the babies? Why? I ask myself as I mourn for the loss of the babies and their families. The babies didn't get the chance to grow up, but I grew up and I need to turn my grandmother's wrong into a right.

Walking out of Yad VaShem ready to carry out a plan I've given much thought to, I head over to a bench in hopes of gathering my composure. Looking back at the museum I realize that not only am I fully connected emotionally, I have now gained a connection physically and spiritually within myself and to the Jewish people. The exhaustingly hard work of healing is finally breaking apart the years of my self-contained imprisonment in a way that is purely human; this connection is now in my bones.

The following day, I wake up early to execute my plan of putting to rest my grandmother's evil words and turning her wrong into a right. I shower, put on my clothes, and head into the kitchen of Pamela's apartment to fix myself a cup of tea. I walk out on the terrace with my mint tea and find Pamela reading her newspaper and drinking coffee.

"Are you ready?"

"I'm getting there."

"Good. You know where to go and you have the phone number in case you get lost," she says as she gets up from the white plastic patio chair to put away her newspaper and walk into the living room.

"Yes, I have the number and I'll call you when it's been done." I take in a deep breath.

"I'm going to work now, if you need anything call me," she said as she gives me a kiss on the cheek.

"I can always count on you for support."

Wearing my white shorts and multi-colored tank top I locate the bus I need to take from the central bus station in Tel-Aviv. I find the bus going to a town named Modiin and get on. Taking the front seat in the air-conditioned bus, I pull out my directions; "Go to the main bus station in Modiin and catch a taxi, then call a man named Elli from the JNF (Jewish National Fund)."

The bus pulls into Modiin, but there is no bus station. All the passengers except one are getting off the bus. I look toward the back and notice a girl with blonde hair has fallen asleep. *Oh dear*, I think to myself, *what am I to do?* I get out my directions and notice the directions say "Mitzpe Modiin."

"Ummm, sir, ummm, I need to go to Mitzpe Modiin," I say softly.

"Mah? (What?)" he responds.

"Can you please take me to Mitzpe Modiin?" I ask.

"Oy v' voy," he says while waving his hands in the air, "why you did not say so?" he asks.

He seems to be agitated and tells me I must stay on the bus, he will drop me off on his way back to Tel-Aviv.

Two hours later the agitated bus driver finally drops me off in the middle of a highway, between Tel-Aviv and Jerusalem. The only thing I have going for me is an orange bus sign that is glued to the top of a stick in the dirt.

The sign provides me with the bus numbers I need to take back to Tel-Aviv. I look around the desert and see a forest across the highway. Running across the highway, I pray no out of control motorist stumbles upon me and turns me into road kill. Making my way across, I proceed to walk up a path that leads me to a sign that reads "Ben Shemen Forest." Below the lettering is the "JNF" logo. I am so relieved.

I pull out my cell phone and call Elli to notify him I have arrived. He tells me to stay put; he will come and get me in eight minutes. I find a picnic table where I sit to wait. Twenty-eight minutes later Elli drives up in a blue Toyota with a wobbling wheel on the driver's side. I get in and thank him for picking me up with a vehicle with air-conditioning. Elli, a tall, dark-haired man, drives approximately two minutes and stops in front of a picnic table in the dirt. He announces we are at the planting site. Laughing, I tell him I could have just walked. Pulling off my seat belt to get out of the car, Elli insists I cool off with the air-conditioning. He offers me a bottle of lemonade from a cooler in the back seat.

"Would you like to see the forest?"

"Sure, I would love to see the forest."

Driving through the forest, I cool off from the heat while Elli begins telling me the story of the cypress and the Lebanon cedar trees.

"When a baby girl is born," he says, "the father plants a cypress tree because it is more modest. Its leaves cover the trunk of the tree."

Elli takes a drink of his cola and continues,

"When a baby boy is born, his father will plant the cedar tree because it is less modest and shows its trunk," he says.

"Then when the girl and the boy grow up and go off to marry the father will cut down the trees and make the chuppah (wedding canopy) from the them," he says as we drive back to the picnic table.

"What a wonderful story." Opening the car door I notice the selection of baby trees huddled together near the picnic table.

Elli informs me of my choices of trees, a cypress or a pine. Remembering his story, I choose a cypress tree, because it represents a girl. I pick a nice healthy-looking one from the bunch.

As we walk over to the area of the forest that had holes already dug for planting, Elli asks, "Who are you planting this tree for?"

"I'm planting this tree in my grandmother's name for all who perished in the Holocaust," I tell him as we stop at the holes.

"So it's as if your grandmother is planting the tree?"

"Yes, my grandmother is planting the tree through me. I'm turning a wrong into a right." Bending down, I choose the hole in which to plant my tree of life.

"You know, most people who come to the forest plant trees for a loved one, but you are planting this life for everyone from the Holocaust. Why?" he asks.

I tell Elli the story of my grandmother, and why it is so important for me to right her wrong, and why I need to bury her words as I plant this tree. Elli then kneels down next to the hole and asks me if I need help reciting the prayer for tree planting. I tell him I want to say the prayer in Hebrew before I plant the tree, then in English, but I need his help with the Hebrew. So I kneel down next to the hole, and, repeating after Elli, I recite the tree-planting prayer in Hebrew.

I put the tree in the hole and begin to cover it with dirt. I immediately begin to feel the weight of her words from so long ago lift away from my body. Standing from the ground, I begin the prayer in English, "I'm planting this tree of life in my grandmother's name, Elizabeth, for all those who perished in the Holocaust."

Heavenly Father, thou who buildest Zion and Jerusalem,
Take pleasure in Thy land,
and bestow upon it of Thy goodness and Thy grace
Give dew for a blessing, and cause beneficent rains
to fall in the mountains of Israel, and her valleys,

and to water thereon every plant and tree.
And these saplings which we plant before thee this day;
Make deep their roots and wide their crown,
that they may blossom forth in grace
amongst all the trees in Israel, for good and for beauty.
And strengthen the lands of all our brethren,
who toil to receive the sacred soil and bless,
o Lord, their might, and may the work of their hands
find favor before Thee.
Look down from Thy holy habitation,
from heaven and bless this land that it may flow again
with milk and honey, Amen.

I said this with a profound sense of relief, as I look up at Elli, standing near me looking at the freshly planted tree of life.

"You're an amazing woman," he said. A tear fell from behind his sunglasses.

"It's done, now my grandmother and her words can rest in peace." I fold the prayer and place it into my pouch.

"Would you like to take a picture?" Elli asks.

"I think not, Elli."

"I know it is here growing, and someday when I tell my children this story they may come to visit this forest."

Walking back to the picnic table, Elli pulls out a certificate and hands it to me.

"Thank you Elli, I appreciate all your help; you are a kind gift." Getting back into the blue Toyota and driving back to the bus stop, Elli proceeds to tell me he wished he could drive me back to Tel-Aviv himself, but he has a new group coming. As I hug him at the bus stop, I can sense his kindness for people.

Sitting on the bus headed for Tel-Aviv I think about how this story took twenty-eight years to come full circle. I'm tired. I know why I feel so tired. I'm tired from carrying the burden for so many years. I feel a great need to honor my tiredness. Looking out the window, I think to myself, *it's over.*

Then looking back down at my hands, I notice their cleanliness and how nicely folded together they are, as if to comfort each other. *Maybe this is what forgiveness is supposed to feel like? Maybe forgiveness is really an emotion and not a conscious choice. This certainly feels like a form of forgiving.*

Chapter 8

The Play

The Trigger — 2002

"I don't wanna grow up! I'm never gonna grow up!" A fifth grade blond-haired boy, playing the part of Peter Pan yelled from the school stage.

We're sitting on blue folding chairs in the gymnasium of Scott and Stephen's elementary school. My husband, Steve, and my son, Stephen, were with me; Scott's fifth-grade class was performing the play.

"Where's Scott, Mommy?" Stephen asked.

"He's playing one of the Lost Kids," I whispered, leaning over close to Stephen's ear.

"Can I go sit with my friends on the floor in front?"

"Sure," Steve answered.

I smiled at Stephen as he made his way over to the front of the stage. He nodded to me when he reached the front, as if to say he made it safely.

I turned my attention back to the stage just in time to watch Scott come from behind the curtain singing, "We'll never grow up."

I laughed and craned my neck to get a closer look between the heads of two parents in front of me, snapping a picture as I experienced a flash of sadness and felt a sense of warmth to my cheeks.

Taking a deep breath I looked over at Steve, who was laughing with the audience. I cracked a smile as I began to feel my head warm up again, with the feeling of humiliation. I breathed slowly in an effort to get rid of the overheated disgraceful feeling.

Then it dawned on me, what I was feeling was a sense of shame. Shame always feels warm, lonely and sad, almost as if shame is an emotion *and* a temperature. Suddenly I felt a great desire to close my jacket and cover my chest with my purse. Leaning my head down into my lap, I rubbed my forehead with the tips of my fingers.

God not now, why now? I just want to be a normal person for just one hour. Why does everything have to be PTSD related? I don't want a flashback now, I just want to enjoy my own child's play – leave me alone. God I'm sick of this shit.

At that moment the flashback appears in front of me. I remember myself in a school play when I was in sixth grade.

Quickly, shaking off the overwhelming pout-like feeling that plagued my mouth and eyes, I placed my hands on my purse telling myself to stop playing that horrific scene. *Now is not the friggin time!*

Taking control of my flashback, I turned to look at the stage and cocked my head as I began dissociating my mind into the play. I'm not about to let the flashbacks control me anymore. *I have an ability to dissociate, and here is one of those times I'm purposely using this survival tool to experience my son's big day.*

For the duration of my son's play, I was successful in pushing the flashback away. But, that night, while lying in bed, the flashes came like little flickers of a movie. All snuggled in my pillow, the epiphany to honor these flashbacks came at me as

I realized I could no longer fight what wants to be freed, thus, allowing the release of my terrified memory and scared emotions.

* * *

The Memory...

The year is 1977 and my best friend, Ann, and I are passing funny-face notes to each other.

Our teacher, Mrs. Anderson, is announcing a new assignment. "OK, class, I'm handing out an assignment that involves a play. You will be divided into groups and will be performing the play for the class. The play must be about someone or something famous."

I lean over and whisper to Ann. "I'm so excited. I love to act."

"Holly, pretending to be Barbra Streisand and singing that ridiculous song you love is not acting. 'Second Hand Rose' is not going to be in our play."

"You're just jealous because you don't have that album."

"Holly, my mom has the record, and I'm not jealous."

"No way! I feel jealous now."

Even though I'm extremely shy, I love acting. I really believe this is the only way I can truly express myself, although I'm not very good at it.

Ann and I get paired up together with two other girls. I feel so lucky to have Ann in my group. I don't know the other kids in my class very well. Ann is my only and best friend. We became friends in fourth grade when I moved to this school after my parents divorced.

I stay the night at Ann's house every chance I can get. Her house is big and beautiful and has a lot of rooms for us to play in. It's the most beautiful home I've ever seen. Her mom is very nice and her dad is funny, always making silly faces at us. Her mom lets us make poached eggs whenever we want.

"Pssst, Ann do you think we can practice the play at your house?" I whisper.

"Oh yeah, we can practice at my house. I'll talk to the other girls and see if we can set up a time."

"Ok, I just don't know the other girls like you do, and I've only been to your house."

"Don't worry about it Holly, we can practice at my house. I bet their moms will be okay with it."

All of us agree to work on our play at Ann's house after school the next day. We only have one day to do our play, but as always, Ann has to ask her mother to drive me home. I always hate that part of going to Ann's house; I always feel as though I'm a burden to Ann's mother because my mother doesn't drive.

Full of excitement, I run home and tell my mother about the play. I know my mother won't help with any ideas, so I don't bother to ask her. If I did ask, she'd tell me she was too busy working her fingers to the bone to put food on the table. She is fond of reminding Marcia and me how lucky we are to have her. I hear that all time, so I don't ask. This time I'm grateful to have Ann in my group because I know her mom will give us ideas.

The next morning I walk into the living room of the apartment and head over to my mother, who is sitting in the red velvet chair next to the big patio window. I walk over to stand next to Marcia as I bend down to give my mother a kiss and collect my forty-five cents for lunch.

"I want you girls to come straight home from school," she says, "No playing around, you hear me, come straight home."

"Huh," Marcia and I simultaneously say standing there in our matching blue overalls, shocked that she forgot about practicing at Ann's house.

"I have to go to Ann's house to practice the play," I remind her with a sense of importance. "I told you about the play last night after you got home from work, don't you remember?"

"Well… that's too bad. Your father is coming here to pick you up and take you to the doctor. You wanna make him mad?" she says, pointing her finger at me.

"Why do we have to go to the doctor?" Marcia asks.

"You both have to get school physicals or the school will kick you out," she says, putting a quarter and two dimes in Marcia's hand.

"Can you ask Dad if he can take me to Ann's house after the doctor's appointment?"

"I'll talk to him, now get out, and remember come straight home, you *don't* want to upset your father," she barks while we rush out the front door.

The other girls will get a head-start on the play without me. They might not even have a part for me once they start working on the play. Everything always gets ruined because of my parents. I hate them! I'm always embarrassed because of them. I want to scream!

As Marcia and I walk to school, she starts to complain about going to the doctor. Marcia doesn't like shots, and nether do I, but I can't think about that right now; I am mad and hurt.

"We've never had to have a physical before, why do we have to have one now?" Marcia asks, stumbling while walking and talking at the same time.

"How am I supposed to know? I can't even remember ever going to the doctor," I respond.

"Yeah, we could be bleeding to death and they wouldn't ever take us to the doctor, so how come the school is making us see one now?"

"I don't know, maybe they changed the rules."

Running into the school, I see a glimpse of Ann standing with the other girls from our group in front of the dark-brown lockers. I look at Marcia and tell her to meet me at the blacktop as soon as the bell rings. I walk up to the girls and explain the situation with the doctor. I tell Ann my father will drive me to her house as soon as the appointment is over, even though I hate the idea of my father squealing his tires onto Ann's driveway.

After school, Marcia and I find each other on the blacktop and without saying a word to each other we immediately take off running for home. We both know not to keep our father waiting, and we know Barbra is not there to make an excuse for us if we're late. Barbra ran off to live with a blond hippie and ended up having a baby, so we can't rely on her to keep Dad busy until we get home.

Sprinting in front of the apartment complex, we see our father sitting in his dirt brown Duster, reading the newspaper. *Shit, we're dead.* Making a dash for the car, my torn up pink book bag drops off my shoulder and onto the pavement.

"Pick it up, hurry!" Marcia yells, running.

"Sorry," I whisper, nervously stumbling over my shoes.

Marcia and I get right into the back seat breathing hard and speechless.

"Hey girls, how was your day?" Dad asks.

"Good," Marcia and I respond simultaneously.

"Holly, your mother called, she said I'm supposed to drop you off at Ann's house. Is that correct?"

"Yeah."

"The word is YES. Yeah is not a word. How many God-damn times do I have to beat that into your fucking head?"

"Sorry. I mean 'yes.'"

"Yes, what?"

"Yes, Sir."

During the drive to the doctor's office, my father gives his lecture on the proper use of the word "yes" as he tells us what fucking idiots we are. I look over at Marcia and roll my eyes; she looks at me with saucer-sized eyes, the scared look face, I call it. She knows if I'm caught rolling my eyes I'm going to get slapped. My father has a way of slapping us while he drives. *He only went to seventh grade, what does he know about proper use of anything?*

We drive up to the doctor's office with the car coming to an abrupt halt. We follow our father into the doctor's office. Dad points to bright red plastic chairs, a sign for Marcia and me to take a seat. We both sit down while Dad walks up to the counter to check us in with the receptionist. Neither of us says a word. *No doubt he'll call her honey, sugar or sweetheart*, I think. *How embarrassing.*

The wait seems like an eternity as I sit waiting to be called. *I hope this goes fast. I've got to get to Ann's house.* The only thing I can think about is Ann and the girls working on the play without me. I look over at Marcia and twiddle my thumbs.

A middle-aged woman comes out from behind a closed door wearing a white uniform, calling our names. Marcia and I stand up and head over to her. I notice my father walking with us as the nurse motions us to enter a room. All three of us—my father, my sister and me—walk into the examining room. The nurse says she'll be back with the doctor. She gives us a sympathetic look by raising her eyebrows together and closing the door behind her as she goes.

I'm a little uncomfortable with both my father and my sister in the same examining room as me. I figure when the doctor comes in, he'll kick those two out.

I'm still thinking about the play when the nurse opens the door and walks in, the doctor following close behind. The doctor, a tall man with gray hair, explains to my father that he has a choice; he can stay in the examining room while he examines me and Marcia, or he can leave and the nurse will stay. I look over at my father, eyes wide. *God, I hope he tells him the nurse can stay, please say the nurse can stay.*

"I'll stay. I want to make sure everything is okay," my father responds, looking down at me and smiling. Marcia and I look at each other as if to say, *this is not right!* I feel like crying. *I want to die, please God just strike me dead. I can't have my father see me naked, I can't. I just can't.*

I'm horrified and scared, and I know the doctor is going to want me to remove my clothes, *but in front of my father? What kind of freak is this doctor? Oh no, I have a training bra on for gawd sakes and he will see it.*
I begin to breathe heavily. I can't swallow. I feel like I'm choking. I look over at Marcia; her face is beet red. I know she feels the same as I do, but I know she's more worried about me; she knows I'm wearing my training bra. *I wish to be a bug, I want to be a bug, God please turn me into a bug. A bug can crawl away. I'll just crawl away.*
I no longer think about the play. I'm in shock. If I run out, my father will for sure grab me by my hair and drag me back in.
"Who wants to go first?" The doctor asks.
Marcia points to me. I know better than to argue while my father is standing right next to me. The room is not very big. It's a tough squeeze for all four of us to be in here.
"Alright Holly, take off your clothes and put this paper dress on. I'll walk out as you get undressed," the doctor instructs.
"Turn around, Dad." I'm imploring him, tears welling up in my eyes.
"I'll turn my back so you can undress."
Dad turns his back and Marcia does the same. I begin taking off my clothes, folding my underwear and my training bra up in my clothes, so no one will see. I slip on the scratchy paper dress as fast as I can.
The doctor walks back into the room and tells me to hop up onto the table. I do, and as soon as I sit up on the table my father and Marcia turn back around to face me. My anguish almost overwhelms me as I look away from Marcia and my father, while they both stand at the foot of the examining table.
The doctor directs me to scoot back on the table. I scoot back and he checks my eyes with a bright light, then my ears.

Then he checks my breathing on my back with his cold metal stethoscope. He places the cold instrument under my paper dress, checking my breathing on my chest. I jump from the invasion and take a deep breath, while Marcia and my father stand against the white concrete wall watching me.

The doctor tells me to lay back. I do holding my paper dress down on my legs. Without warning, the doctor lifts my hands and puts them on my chest; lifting my paper dress he tells me to spread my legs. Blood rushes to the top of my head. I feel faint and foggy as I feel myself float away from my body. All sound becomes muffled.

I feel like melting into the examining table, and then I freeze. I clap my legs together, feeling my father watch down there. Again, the doctor tells me I need to spread my legs a little so he can check me. I take a hard swallow, closing my eyes tightly. My lips quiver as the realization of my father at the end of the table watching me, I silently cry inside my body. Spreading my legs, my mind begins to rush questions through my brain. *Check me? Check me for what? I don't ever remember a doctor checking my privates before, why do I need to be checked now?* I want to burst out the questions as I lay in my torment, but I can't speak. I can hardly swallow now, and I know my father is still standing at the end of the table watching, seeing, glaring down at my privates. *How can he do this too me? How can he allow this? How can this be happening? Fuckers, I hate them, I hate them all.*

The doctor takes his hands and spreads my legs further apart; touching my vagina he pulls the skin on each side. I feel his hands probing; I feel him breathing; I try focusing on the ceiling above me as I pray for this nightmare to end. But it doesn't. The doctor tells me to sit up and turn over. I sit up feeling mortified, I look at my father, his face is dark red. I look over at Marcia, who has averted her eyes and is looking down at the speckled linoleum floor.

I turn over on the table like the doctor asks; I try to hold the back of the paper dress together. Lying on my stomach I hold my head straight down on the table; forehead leaning on the table. The doctor proceeds to take my hand off the paper dress. I hold it tight; he tries to pull my fingers from the dress.

"Holly, you have to let go, I need to check back here now," he states.

"Why?" I ask while looking down at the paper on the table beneath me.

"Holly, let the doctor do his job," my father says, his voice tight. He's obviously annoyed.

I hate you, I hate you all, I HATE you! I release my grip on the gown and place my small fists to the sides of me. The doctor pulls the two sides of the dress apart, exposing my backside. I feel very cold and begin to shiver. He pulls my butt cheeks apart. I throw my hands up towards my face and slap them on my eyes as I raise my head. I am embarrassed, ashamed and humiliated as my mind floats me to the top of the gray filing cabinet next to the window. There I sit and watch, but I can't stay long because I'm jolted by the doctor's voice, then my father.

"Okay Holly, you can get up," the doctor says.

"Holly, you can get up," he says again.

"Holly!" My father shouts.

I swing my legs around and sit up, my long curly brown hair in my face. I grab at the paper dress to cover myself and look over at my father. His face is not only beet red, he is swallowing hard; I can see his Adam's apple bob looking lumpy as he swallows.

The doctor moves my hands again from the paper dress and checks my ribs from the back then proceeds to press on my breasts. Pressing and squishing with the palms of his big, cold hands. After pressing on my breasts, the doctor takes out his knee-jerking stick to check my reflexes.

"Okay, you're done."

"Marcia your turn," My father says.

"Huh?" Marcia looks up at me in that same scared face look as before.

"Here is a paper dress for you Marcia, I'll be back," the doctor says.

"Turn around, Dad." I say, spit spraying as I jump off the table.

My father turns his back and I dress while Marcia undresses. I know the doctor will do to her what he just did to me, and I am dying to leave the room, but I know Marcia doesn't want me to leave. I walk between my father and the examining table, keeping my head down, looking at the floor. I position myself to be as far away from him as I can get. I lean against the filing cabinet and keep my eyes on the floor as Marcia goes through the same exam. I refuse to watch, but I hear the doctor making the same requests to her as he did me. I hear her paper dress and the paper on the table rustle as she switches positions for him. *I want to just go home, crawl under my blanket and die. I don't want to be a part of this world, I hate this world; this world is cruel and mean and I hate the way I feel. I hate the way I live and I hate everyone around me. I don't want to go to Ann's house anymore; I just want to go home.*

Once Marcia's examination is finished we head back toward the waiting area. My father goes to the counter and Marcia and I walk outside and get in the car. We don't speak. I don't feel like talking, and neither does Marcia. We both hold our heads down as my father gets into the driver's seat. During the drive, we are all silent; he doesn't even yell at any of the other drivers.

As we pull up to Ann's house, I begin feeling guilty for leaving Marcia with Dad. I open the car door and get out without saying a word. As I approach Ann's big beautiful house I notice the smell of freshly cut grass. I ring the doorbell and Ann's mother opens the door, a big smile on her face.

"Hi, Holly. The girls are downstairs waiting for you."

"Thanks, Mrs. Harrison, I'll find them," I respond solemnly, knowing I sound sad and hope she doesn't ask why.

"Are you excited to do the play?" Mrs. Harrison asks, seeing me into the kitchen.

"Sure." I head toward the basement door.

"The girls have been giggling ever since they got here from school. I'm sure they'll be glad you're here."

I head downstairs with a lump in my throat. I see the girls and Ann laughing and dancing. Ann drops her black feather boa and runs over to me, telling me about the musical she and the girls have choreographed together. She jumps up and down with excitement as the girls dance and laugh to the 1930s style music. I see how excited she is, but I can't hear her. I feel like I'm in a daze as I take a seat on her tattered brown sofa. I glance over at the two other girls and watch as they dance. I see how they have all their steps down; they've been practicing. I look up at Ann, who is still going on and on about the musical.

"Holly, are you listening?"

"Uh huh," I sputter, shaking myself out of my dreamlike state.

"Holly, the musical is for three performers, but we'll make you a part, ok?"

"Yeah, sure. I don't feel like having much of a part anyway." My heart feels broken.

I just want to go home. I can crawl under my blanket and die. I hate this place. I don't want to be here. I don't want to be anywhere. I hate it here.

"Ok, now just sit and watch us and tell me what you think." Ann throws me a glowing smile.

"OK."

"We're going to do the play for you, and if you like it you can stand next to me doing the same part, alright?" she says restarting the record player.

Sitting here watching them dance and sing, the room begins to close in and look foggy. I began to feel overwhelmingly sad and bust out in tears. I start sobbing, my windpipe beings to swell, I can't breathe. I put my head down and fall into the coach.

"We don't have to do this play; we can make a different play." Ann has raised her voice over the music, obviously concerned.

"Don't cry, Holly, we can make a new play," Tammy, one of the other girls, says.

"Yeah, don't cry about it," Sara says, "We can change it."

"I can't do it, I wish I can be like you guys, but I can't. It will never be for me." I cover face with my hands.

Tammy turns off the music and Ann sits down next to me. Ann explains how we can change the play, because she doesn't want to upset me. Looking over my shoulder at her and trying to compose myself to utter out a few words, I explain that's not the reason I'm crying. Rubbing my back she asks, "What is the matter then?"

"I can't tell you." I push my hair from my face.

"Please Holly, what's the matter?" she begs as the girls stand around looking down at me.

"I'll be fine. I just need to use the bathroom."

"Yeah, want us to work on another play?" Sara asks.

"No, I'll be fine. We can do what you've worked on." I head into the bathroom.

Following me to the bathroom, Ann hands me a washcloth. I tell her that I'm fine and I'll learn the steps to the play.

"Are you sure?"

"Yeah, everything will be better tomorrow when we do the play for the class."

I managed to disconnect myself from my hurt feelings and learn the steps to the musical. Ann, Tammy, Sara and I reenacted our play the following day for our class, and I hid behind a disguise. I felt even more different from everyone else, and I knew why. The small spirit I had then was diminished even further into the pit of my gut after that doctor's visit.

To this day, I have no doubt my father had Marcia and me checked for sexual activity by that doctor. I was 12 and Marcia was 10. The following two years I would see less and less of my father until one day he never came back around. Then, right after my 14th birthday, my mother moved Marcia and me to Las Vegas. That move would forever change my life.

* * *

A Healing Story....

Virginia Woolf once wrote, "I thought how unpleasant it is to be locked out; and I thought how it is worse, perhaps, to be locked in." This is an inspirational quote I keep with me as I write.

Where does the pain go once it's written? When I began my journey to heal I started by writing. Although, I soon realized I didn't know how to write. I mean, I could write, but not with the skill of a true writer, one who writes with poise and shows a masterful way of stringing words together.

It all started when I went to Israel for the first time. I felt alive and free from the demons that lurked within the confines of my mind. I bought a postcard, and like a schoolgirl began to write of my adventures. I wrote about my volunteer work and meeting soldiers. Fitting tiny, hand-written words on my postcard, I told of the bus trips I took, and the ancient places I visited. I was filled with delight and happiness as I wrote it all down, giving myself something to remember my trip by.

Then when I finished writing, I kissed my postcard, licked the stamp and placed it in the corner. Just then, I remembered that I had no parents to send this postcard. The realization hit me like a ton of bricks as I sat on the edge of a curb, addressing the postcard to them. I had been writing with excitement and passion, telling my mother of my first experiences in Israel.

That realization and pain led me down a healing path of journaling my stories of the past.

"This hurts!" I yell. "I don't want to do this anymore; it's too painful."

Tears are streaming down my cheeks. I wipe my nose with my sleeve as I get up from my red chair, pacing the floor of my home office. Back and forth I walk on the cream colored carpet while running my small fingers through my thick brown hair. My right arm feels as though it weighs a hundred pounds. I know the physical pain in my arm is there because, through my writing, I've disturbed some deep hurt from the caverns inside my gut, and now it's moving through my arm and out onto the keyboard.

I sit back down on my swivel chair and stare at the computer screen, concentrating intensely. I flip though my Word documents and read all the stories I've written; I force myself to read the painful truth. To see the abuse I endured, and the ugliness in it all. Through my words, I look into the effects and the hard work in healing I've done. I sit here examining my stories, my life, my emotions, as I feel my words speak with honest clarity.

The art in writing as a healing tool is that the truth doesn't lie. It's there on paper; the facts open up and evolve as I write each of my stories, bringing validation to the wounded self that carries the horrors.

Writing supports me as I walk down this path of healing, and it enables me to feel my feelings in black and white. It allows me to flush out the self-consumption of the abuse, along with the effects it's had on my life and me.

As I've witnessed, there is something liberating and cathartic about writing to heal. Whether it's a brilliant poem, or raw paragraphs, telling the story through writing can mend shattered wounds, thus releasing poisonous pain.

It all started with a postcard, which I still have, and so today, I'm able to honor myself through writing, because of what I wrote down yesterday.

Chapter 9

The Broom

The Trigger…

The dream was frantic. *Run, run, run! You need to hurry! Hurry, get out of there. Go! Get out of the wooded darkness. You're going too slow; she's going to catch you! Move girl, move!*
Breathe, Holly, breathe, just-- got to -- keep -- running, I tell myself, twisting my body up in my heavy blankets. Where's my bottle of Pepto-Bismol? I need the Pepto-Bismol.
Look on the ground, search, search, faster, faster, she'll see you.
But I need it…It's my tummy medicine.
Find it then, but hurry. I don't want her to catch us.
"Where the hell are you? I'm sick of you rotten kids trying to destroy my life! Do you hear me? I'm sick of it," Mom screams.
Hurry, Holly! I see her waving that big stick in the air. You're gonna get hurt, you're gonna get hurt, you're gonna get hurt….
Wake up Holly; get up… move your eyelids.
Where's my Pepto-Bismol? I need it, it helps my anxiety. Please, I need it. I'll run to my boyfriend's house, that's where I'll run; she

can't hurt me there. He'll keep me safe, he'll make me feel better, it'll be better, better, better...

Move your ass out of the darkness, you're gonna get hurt! Stop crying, what's the matter now? Look, I see your Pepto-Bismol, pick it up, run. The stick, Holly, she's got that stick.

"You kids are always trying to destroy my life, it is all your fault Holly Dawn. It's all your fault! You just couldn't go to school and do as you were told, no Holly Dawn, you couldn't you had to go off at the age of fourteen and become an alcoholic just like your father, you fucking little selfish bitch, always trying to destroy me," Mom screams as she pounces through the dark forest, soaring as if she has springs on her feet.

Grab the bottle, Holly; the springs on her feet are turning into big spider legs. Run, Holly, run! The nutty bitch is gonna catch us. Move your ass, girl!

I'm not an alcoholic; I hate spiders, why's she calling me an alcoholic? I only tried it that one time. Ah, there's the Pepto-Bismol bottle. Grab it.

I can't make out the voices; they're all a big loud blur, they're muffled. The forest is dark and I run to my boyfriend's house. I bang hard on the door with my fist, but he won't let me in. Finally, he opens the door and tells me to go to the bedroom.

I toss and turn, pulling the blankets to my chin, feeling sick to my stomach. My eyes flutter as I try to move myself out of the quicksand of nightmares, but I can't quite manage it. I need to escape, to run. I hear Mom's voice screaming, echoing.

He's not safe Holly. Remember Holly? Remember? You need to remember, you must remember! Run Holly, run!

I'm in his room, it's dark, and lights are flashing through the blinds. I hear leaves rustle outside. Something is coming. Mom's scream echoes through the window. "You're trying to kill me! It's you! You're a selfish girl, Holly. You're a selfish little girl. You left the electrical plugs in the wall so the house will burn down and kill me in the middle of the night. You left your hair dryer plugged in again! You are all trying to kill me, trying to destroy me."

I hear my name being called, but I can't answer back. I strain to open my eyes and toss my leaden body. I pull at my ears. The voice keeps calling, low, just outside the dream.

"Wake up Holly, wake up."

Run to Israel, Holly. It's safe in Israel, run, run. She thinks you're trying to destroy her, Holly. She's always thought this, always. Holly, she's whacked. Holly! Get up and run.

"Holly, Holly, wake up, wake up."

Fucking electrical plugs again! If I hear one more damn shit thing about those fucking electrical cords, I'm gonna throw 'em in the trash. What's her problem with those things anyway? I'm scared to run, I'm scared they'll hurt me if I run. I'm terrified, I'm bad if I run. I'm rotten to the core if I run.

Holly, she's got a screw loose, now run. It's safe to run. Please, Holly, let's not get hurt anymore. He doesn't love you. Run, Holly, run. Think of the sweet smell of Israeli air. Think of your children, how much you love your children, run to see your children. Holly, run to the people and places you love. Run, Holly, run away from the craziness.

"HOLLY, WAKE UP!"

I open my eyes and look up to see Steve leaning over me, shaking me.

"Huh, what?"

"You're making a lot of noise again. Another nightmare?"

"Ummm, no, not yet, just one of those same yucky ones.

*   *   *

The Memory…

It's 1979, I'm fourteen now and our move to Las Vegas is exciting. Marcia and I are giggly and happy, but my feeling for Mom goes sour. I start to resent her for always protecting him, bringing him up in our faces, telling us we act like him when we're bad.

We move into a two-bedroom townhouse. Mom takes a job at a beauty salon. She takes a bus to work. Marcia and I start school at the junior high across the street, where I make two friends very quickly, Mary and Kristina. Mary lives far away and takes a bus to school, but Kristina lives within walking distance, and sometimes I go to her house after school to do homework.

Today Kristina invites me over. She asks me if I can stay late because her parents are out of town. Her brother won't be home until after dark and she doesn't want to stay home by herself. I'm so excited at the invitation, and even though I know I will have to walk home in the dark, I agree.

When we get to Kristina's house I call home and tell Marcia where I am so Mom won't go ballistic when she finds out I'm not home.

Kristina and I play basketball on the concrete drive in the sun. I'm pretty good for as short as I am. Being small has never really bothered me. I'm used to always being the smallest in school. Besides, I know all the rules.

After playing a few games, Kristina and I head into the kitchen for a snack and some lemonade. Walking by the bar from the kitchen, Kristina asks if I've ever tasted wine before.

"No, I don't think that stuff's good for you," I say, thinking of my father and all the times he drank too much. "Have you ever tasted it?" I ask, taking a bite of a peanut butter and jelly sandwich.

"Nope, but I think I'm going to try it."

"Ewww. You are?"

"Sure, why not? Might be fun."

I hate the thought of alcohol, but I can't tell Kristina that, she might think I'm weird or something.

We walk over to the bar while we eat our sandwiches. She pulls out a bottle that's inside a small refrigerator under the counter, and a glass from the cabinet next to it. She fills a glass and takes a sip, her lips puckering instantly. She hands me the glass and tells me to try it. *What do I do? I can't let her think anything's wrong or she'll ask questions.*

Holding the short glass; I smell it. *It smells like Dad.* "Na, it smells gross. I'm not gonna drink it."

"What? OK, fine, I know what we can try." She pours the wine down the tiny bar sink and pulls out a bottle of Kahlua. She pours the brown thick liquid into the same short glass.

"My parents always mix this with milk," she says, pulling out a short carton of milk and adding a few splashes to the liquor. She hands me the glass, I squint my eyes shut and hover my lips over the rim. With one quick motion I take a big sip. Surprisingly I find the concoction to be smooth and yummy.

I lick my lips. "Not bad." I hand the glass back to Kristina, who takes a sip.

"Yummmm, that's good," she agrees. "Let's make more."

We decide to make full size glasses of the mixture, and soon after having drunk the whole glass, I feel light-headed and sick. We clean up our mess and head over to the back door. It's time for me to go and I head out the back to walk home.

Swaying side to side, I walk home feeling queasy and scared. As I approach my front door, I immediately feel a rush of fear in my throat. I take a hard swallow and decide the best thing for me to do is to act sick and head straight up to my room. It sounds perfectly rational. *She won't know I was drinking alcohol if I stay far away from her.*

I open the front door and stagger into the living room. I remember my father's eyes whenever he came home drunk. His eyes were always red from the alcohol, and I just know my eyes are that way, too. I take a quick glance into the living room and see Mom sitting on the hand-me-down white velvet couch. Marcia is sitting on the floor, watching T.V.

I swiftly walk in front of the T.V. right over to the light switch that's near the stairs. I turn the stair lights off and race upstairs, turning the other lights off as I walk down the hall. I can hear my mother's voice holler behind me.

"What's wrong with her?"

I run into my bedroom and roll out my blankets to make a bed on the floor. We don't have any bedroom furniture because Mom sold it before we moved. I grab my pillow from the closet and fall onto my homemade bed. The room begins to spin all around me and I can hear my mother's voice echoing throughout the house. I can't make out the words, but I know she's complaining about something. I roll over and bury my head into my pillow in hopes of drowning out the noise. My head is throbbing and feels strangely thick. *I hope she isn't going to want to lecture us in the middle of the night again about one of us wanting to kill her by leaving the plugs in the wall.*

I doze off and waken to my sister Marcia whispering from the doorway. "Pssttt! Holly, Mom wants you to come downstairs. She thinks there's something wrong with you."

I roll over and look at the doorway, blurry to my slightly tipsy eye.

"Tell her I'm sick, or somethin'. I don't feel good. I just wanna to go to sleep."

"Get your ass down here right now!" Mom screams from the bottom of the stairs. Marcia jumps at the echo and says softly, "See? You need to go down there."

I drag myself to standing and, before I know it, my mother is standing in the doorway of my bedroom.

"What the hell have you been doing? Have you been taking drugs? You've been drinking!" she screams, grabbing me by the hair. "I can smell it."

"I'm sorry, I'm sorry, I will never do it again." I plead, crying out. Marcia runs downstairs and Mom pushes me down, kicking me in the stomach and punching me in the shoulders, head and face.

"You're just like your fuckin' father, a drunk! I got rid of an alcoholic, but you're just like him. I'll get rid of you, too."

"I'm sorry, I'm sorry, please stop!"

Mom tires out and backs off. I pick myself up off the floor and begin explaining.

"We were only experimenting," I explain, snot dripping from my nose. "I only wanted to taste it."

Mom grabs my Urban Cowboy knockoff shirt with an iron grip, tugging me closer and then smacking me in the head. She drags me out into the hall, yelling constantly.

"Now I'm going to be up all fucking night because of you, so you're going to be up with me, you hear? You are going to sit up all night, too!"

"Alright, alright," I whimper, holding my hands over my head for protection from her forceful slaps.

I fall to the floor right above the stairs, where she starts kicking me. I can't keep my balance, the effects of the alcohol and her violence reeling me. I tumble down the flight of stairs, crashing my head against the knee-high wall at the bottom. My head throbs and my vision becomes even more blurry. My ears are ringing, muffling out any sound. *Am I dead?* I float away from my body. I feel calm as I watch myself move from the steps and stagger around. I look around room. Time seems to have completely stopped.

I jolt back into my body when I feel my mother grab a handful of my hair, pulling me down to the floor. I land sharply on my knees, and the force of her kick lifts my fragile, 80-pound body. Marcia screams and begins to cry. Mom kicks me a few more times, getting me in the back and my legs. I roll over and get up to run out. Before I can gain my balance she grabs the back of my shirt again and slaps me a few times in the back of my head.

"You're just like your fucking father, you little bitch!"

"Please stop, stop, stop," I spit out, my hair sticking to the snot on my face, as I feel my breathing shake with fear.

"You are *not* going to come in my home and treat me like this, you hear me!" she yells. "I got news for you, I'll fucking kill you!"

"Let me go! Let me go!" I yell, struggling to break free of her grip on my shirt.

I fall down again and look up to see Marcia curled up on the couch crying, rocking back and forth. Mom tires out again and backs up. I feel her grip release and I stumble to stand and run.

Running toward the front door I reach for the knob when I feel an agonizing pain run across my back. I fall forward, hitting my cheek on the doorknob.

"Oh my God, *Mom!*" I hear Marcia scream again. I look up at the door. I roll over onto my side, grab my knee and stand up. As I grab the doorknob, I feel another powerful blow run across my back and hear a sickening popping sound. My breath is knocked from me and I fall to the floor again, clawing at my throat. I go numb. All sound ceases and time stops. I look across the floor and see the handle of the busted broom. My mother is screaming and Marcia is sobbing. My mother is holding the other end of the broken broom, her face a caricature of rage.

"How dare you try to ruin my life, you selfish little bitch!"

Opening my eyes wide, I jolt up; grab the doorknob and race out into the dark night.

Running out of the town home complex I dash toward the street, crying, wiping the tears from my eyes. I scurry across the road so fast that I run right into oncoming traffic. Cars screech and horns honk as I dart across the street. My cheek pulsates from the pain of hitting the doorknob and my back throbs deep inside. I run onto the grass and down the hill that leads to a park and baseball field. I see a bench and run over to it. Quivering, I sit down and sob while my head and back pound with pain. I am scared and confused, and I keep looking around the park, even though my vision is still blurry. My legs and arms shake like a jackhammer. My teeth chatter and I can feel blood dripping from my mouth. I cling to the seat of the wooden bench.

Out of the corner of my eye, I notice a dark-colored van with black tinted windows parked on the black top. I look away and notice a small red brick building, the bathroom. *Should I go in the bathroom and hide? I can get some toilet paper and clean up my mouth. No, bad idea. There might be someone lurking in there waiting for a girl like me. No, I won't go in there. Maybe I should go knock on the van window and see if anyone is in there. I'm so stupid; I can't believe I drank that booze. I should have known she would smell it. God, I'm dumb! I'm one dumb, stupid idiot. I should be lucky for everything I have, but no, I have to go ruin everything.*

I look over and see a car coming toward me; I stand up to run.

"Holly is that you?" The car is Mrs. Leonardo's, and she is leaning out the window, yelling. Mrs. Leonardo is our kind old neighbor, she moved out of the town homes soon after we moved in, Mom must've called her.

Great, now everyone will know I screwed up.

"Yes it's me, Mrs. Leonardo." I walk slowly over to her shiny new maroon Cadillac.

"Your mother called and told me you ran out of the house drunk."

"I'm sorry Mrs. Leonardo." Tears run down my face. I'm too ashamed to look her in the eye.

"Get in sweetie, I'll take you home." I freeze from the thought of going back home.

"No, that's OK. I'll stay out here for now. I'll go home on my own, thank you."

"No, dear. I'll take you to my house, now get in," she demands.

I slink into Mrs. Leonardo's car and bend my head down, covering my face with my hair. I place my hands in my lap, tightly folded.

"Your mother told me what happened."

I stare out the window over at the dark van.

"You're bleeding, dear." She hands me a box of tissue.

I wipe my face.

"I'm sorry, Mrs. Leonardo."

"Don't worry about it, honey."

When we get to her house, she brings out blankets and pillows and makes a bed for me on her overstuffed floral sofa.

"I want to explain," I begin, "I've never done anything like that before. This was my first time." I'm so worried what she will think of me, that she will judge me harshly.

"You have nothing to explain. We all try things at some time," she says. "Now don't you worry about a thing. You just get into bed here and go to sleep. We'll work this all out tomorrow," she says, handing me a tube of ointment for my mouth.

My mother and I never talked about that night. My outside wounds healed, though my back still gives me aches every now and then. But my inside wounds feel like sharp pieces of glass. My mother never beat me like that again, and she even lightened up on Marcia. Other forms of punishment were used after that, like withholding food, making us sleep out on the patio, and locking us out of the house, all of which I thought were better than the beatings. We moved shortly after that incident into a two-bedroom apartment across town, and I never touched alcohol again. But, Mrs. Leonardo's high school-aged son introduced me to sex, which lead me to sexual relations with another boy after we moved. Another lesson in a long series of lessons I had to learn the hard way.

*   *   *

A Healing Story...

"Misplaced Identity" 2006

Take my hand, little Holly. I'm the adult version of you and together we are going to heal the inner pain and despair that has trapped you in the darkness of all that abuse.

You poor girl, you never did anything to deserve such treatment. Your mother took all those years of being married to an alcoholic out on you. It was him she was angry at; it was he that tried to ruin her life, not you. Your mother was confused. She chose to take her rage for the way your father treated her out on you. She held you responsible for his actions.

I'm sorry for all the pain, all the hurt that has stayed inside with no release. I know how painful and scary this is for you. I know how the nightmares have plagued your life with sadness, shame and anger. I understand how hard it has been for you to hang on, to go through life in a disguise.

There, there, little one. Cry out the pain; purge yourself of the trauma you have borne. I'll take on some of the burden, Holly, but I can't do it alone. I need you to tell me your feelings. I need you to speak to me, point to where it all hurts. I'll hear you and all the cells in my body will feel the agony you felt but could never express. I'll take on the pain and horror of the nightmares and release them from the graves they've burrowed deep within.

I grieve for you, young girl. I feel your pain at how mother treated you. I feel how sad you are inside, laced with the guilt that was always placed upon you by the very people who brought you into the world. I sense how you long to be accepted and loved. Yes, it hurts, Holly. The blows by your mom and dad to your very existence are killing you inside. I'll show you the love and compassion you deserve. I'll take the lead as the adult and protect and cherish the girl that endured so many traumas.

I'm holding you and being the mother you needed growing up. The grown up me is praising and honoring you, Holly, as the child that needs to continue on our journey to heal the pains of the past.

Together we'll heal all the suffering. Together you and I will banish all the evil that was inflicted upon us.

You did nothing wrong, Holly. They did. You are a precious child who deserves to be protected and cherished. You have so much joy and love inside of you. You are always so full of life and warmth. I will guide you, I will protect you. You and I will go through the hell of this together. We will feel the anger, the rage, the shame, and the sadness. We can do this, Holly. We can pick up the pieces that were shattered inside and glue them back together. It's up to us. I'll always be here protecting you, and never will I let you fall.

I admire and applaud your contributions in life. I am here to provide you with the fortitude to move through the damage that debilitates us at times. I'll be gentle and care for you as you take on the courage to speak the truth. Release the pain; grieve the child to live the life. We can do this. Grab my hand.

Let's go to the swings, after all, it's never too late to give you a happy childhood.

Look at the light, Holly. See the bright, shining light? It's the light of an awakening soul. It's a brilliant glow that penetrates. You are the master of your soul now; it is you who makes this journey possible. Let's always remember to be gentle to ourselves as we tiptoe, skip, and stride down our journey to heal.

Chapter 10

Scared and Lost – Healing Wounds

The Trigger... 2004

"Hola! Hola!" The Costa Rican parrot squawked, while I sung out a Barry Manilow favorite to the colorful bird. "Her name was Lola. She was a showgirl. With yellow feathers in her hair and a dress cut down to there. She would meringue and do the cha-cha...."

I giggle at my own voice and, feeling content, walked out of the little Costa Rican pet store into the humid heat. Momentarily the sun blinds me. I squint and see Steve standing next to an outdoor travel agency.

Steve and I are on vacation and we have ended up in a little town named Tamerindo, just on the North-West Pacific coast of Costa Rica.

"Hey! What are you doing?" I yell as I walked over toward him. He tells me that he's going to look for some local activities for us to do. I decide to let him search the stacks of pamphlets and homemade flyers on his own. I know I'll be okay with whatever he chooses. I decide to kill time by wandering down the quaint dirt road.

As I turn a corner, I hear a man yelling in Spanish. The object of his diatribe is a young teenage girl sitting on concrete steps that lead into a supermarket. The man is looming over her, his voice booming and his finger pointing menacingly at her.

Digging in my purse I walk fumbling for my sunglasses as I head closer toward the noise. The man is dressed in khaki shorts and a dirty white T-shirt with a faded Corona logo on it. I stop across the narrow dirt road from them, and stare. I notice a local woman sitting in a white rusted Toyota station wagon. She is also watching the scene, looking nervous and biting her thumbnail. *I wonder if she is his wife?* The girl is crying, her hands clutched tightly together, and no one other than the lady and I seem to notice.

I can't believe my eyes. The man's face is turning red, his veins are ready to pop out of his forehead, he is screaming at the top of his lungs, and no one seems to care.

I begin to feel faint and dig deeper in my bag for my sunglasses. My head starts to feel fuzzy; my stomach tightens into a knot. Flushes of blood enter my face and my throat feels swollen, a glaze skims over my eyes. I take a step back and hear a loud horn honk. I've taken several steps into the dirt road and am standing right in the middle. Suddenly I lose my orientation; I spin around and dash toward a palm tree on the edge of the dirt road across from the run down supermarket.

I squat down and dig in my purse for my Pepto-Bismol tablets while keeping an eye on the screaming lunatic across the road. I pop two tablets in my mouth and look up to see that the shouting man has somehow begun to resemble my own father.

Squinting my eyes, I take a deep breath and swallow hard. In a flash, the Costa Rican family visually becomes my family. This isn't the first time I've had visual flashbacks, seeing my parents at a glance, when they weren't really there. But this is the first time where a man, I've never seen before visually formed into my father's appearance.

I turn my head and cover my ears as I stand up from crouching in the dirt. My purse dangles from my arm while I briskly walk over toward the beach. Plopping myself onto the sand, I stare off into the ocean. I have always remembered the horrible events of my past, and I've always had bizarre clarity to my memories, but at this moment my mind begins to flood with the appalling visions of my father screaming and honking his horn at my mother to hurry as she would run into the grocery store. Marcia and I would hunker down in the back seat to avoid his scary, nasty rage. The memories of my father picking up women hitchhikers along the road flash through my brain. Marcia and I sat in the back seat watching him make sexual advances toward strange women. He'd put his arm on the back of the seat while calling them "honey." He always called them "honey." I remember how my father would sell cars from the gravel driveway of our house and force Barbra to take test rides with strange men in order to sell the cars. I sometimes was made to go along.

I look back across the dirt road at the wrecked little supermarket and notice the yelling man, the fear stricken crying teen, and the rusted out white Toyota station wagon with the woman inside were all gone. And here I sit, looking at my box of Pepto-Bismol tablets, reliving yet another flashback that needs healing.

*   *   *

The Memory — 1981
"Hey Holly, welcome back to Omaha. Sorry Mom sent you back cuz you're knocked up and all," Barbra says, as we walk through the Omaha airport parking lot. I'm fifteen-years-old now and haven't seen Barbra in a year and half.

"What happened to your eye?" I ask while she drives me to her house.

"Shit happens, ya know? Oh and by the way, the house I live in isn't in that great of shape."

"Whatcha' mean?"

"It's been condemned, okay?" She laughs. I shrug my shoulders in response. *What's condemned mean?*

"So, who's the guy that knocked ya up and how long did you date? Can't be too long, yer only fifteen. Tell me about him." She lights a cigarette.

"His name is Jesse and we've been dating for over a year. He lives with his dad in Vegas. His mom lives in New York with his two brothers and a sister." I sigh and look down at my hands, tightly folded in my lap.

"Well, sorry Holly, but you won't be able to call him."

"Why not? I need to let him know how I'm doing." I respond with a sense of great sadness to my heart.

"Sorry, Holly. I don't have a phone. Things cost money, and I don't have the money for a phone, sorry."

I feel incredibly disgusted and ashamed with myself. I miss my friends and school, but most of all I miss Jesse. I feel the light inside of me close just a little more.

Living with Barbra is no picnic; she seems to always be angry and running out the door. I busy myself with cleaning, caring for her two boys, and working the fleas out of the sofa I'm given to sleep on. Tina, the family dog, has them, too. Barbra took her when we moved to Las Vegas. I'm grateful to have Tina; I feel she's my only friend in all this mess.

Barbra takes me to the doctor once a month and the laundromat every Saturday. Barbra is still with the hippie boyfriend she ran off with. He's gross and often makes sexual advances toward me. It's kind of hard to understand why she ran away from Mom and Dad if she lives the same kind of hell here. I feel sad for her, but I'd never tell her that.

Being pregnant is pretty scary. I don't know what will happen to the baby or me. I know my mom sent me to live with Barbra because she didn't want to deal with my problems, and Barbra is too busy staying gone to talk to me. I feel overwhelmed and scared at times, but at least I have Tina. She always listens and now that I've gotten rid of most of the fleas, I keep her on the couch with me. Most days I stare out the living room window and watch the high school kids walk to school. I wish things could be different. Living in Barbra's dumpy house and taking care of her two boys is harder than I ever thought. But, I know once the baby is born, I'll go back to Las Vegas and my mom and Jesse will help with the baby and I can go back to school. I try really hard to remember this isn't forever and life will get better as soon as the baby comes.

In April of 1981, my son Sean is born and Mom and Marcia come to visit. I'm so confused; having a baby is a lot more work than I thought and I feel to get through each day is a struggle emotionally. I feel really sad all the time and the only thing I can think about is how I'm going to go to school and take care of a baby. I'm excited to go home, I want to go home and start back at school, but Mom decides it's best for her to move back to Omaha and save money. This saddens me, I don't want to stay in Omaha, I want to be with Jesse and my friends. Barbra finally gets a phone and I'm able to be in contact with Jesse, although at this point he has grown nasty toward me and he's dating other girls. Feeling rejection from Jesse hurts a lot and makes me feel lonely. He knows I had a baby; we've talked about it several times, yet he doesn't ever offer to help me. He used to always tell me how much he loved me and how he comes from this big Catholic Italian family that's tight and close, yet as time goes on I sense neither he nor his family are all that great.

A couple months after Sean's birth, Mom and Marcia move back to Omaha and Sean and I move in. A year goes by and every so often I talk to Jesse on the phone, but for the most part I know in order to get help from him I need to move back to Las Vegas and ask the courts there for help. Child support enforcement sends him letters every month, but he just ignores them. There's not a lot I can do. I have no money and I'm in a different state than he is. His parents don't seem to care, which is really evil of them.

Mom is saving money so we can move back and I'm working at Pizza Hut as a waitress. Marcia goes to school and is dating this guy who lives in our townhouse community. Needless to say, she has no desire to move back to Las Vegas.

Six months later, we start packing the house for our move back to Vegas and out of the blue Jesse calls. The year is now 1983 and Jesse claims he can't live with himself over his treatment of Sean and me; he's been having nightmares. He's moved back to New York to live with his mom and wants Sean and me to move to New York to be with him. Without even giving the offer much thought, I agree it would be the best thing for Sean. And, despite everything, I miss Jesse. I tell my mother of my plans to move to New York to be with Jesse. Mom hates the idea of Sean and me moving to New York. She tells me every day how that family never helped and never cared. She says the Italians will steal Sean from me and throw me out. She always says once I leave I can never come back. That's really scary for me, but Jesse and I agree to save our money from working and Sean and I will move to New York in May. Despite what my mother says.

Then my world comes crashing down on top of me. Mom starts dating my father again. We haven't heard from him in years and during that time he remarried. Her dating him makes me sick and I try to ignore them. During my wait to move to New York I earn my GED and dream of making plans to attend college when I get there. My father makes fun of my plans and Mom has been allowing him to sleep over. Before I know it, everything falls apart. Marcia ends up pregnant and Barbra leaves her hippie creep boyfriend. Marcia and Barbra are getting a place together and Mom is moving Dad into our town house. The day Dad moves back in is the day my life goes from bad to worse.

"Holly, I'm taking you and Sean for a ride this morning, so get your ass up and ready," Dad barks, standing in the doorway of my bedroom snapping his fingers.

I'm still terrified of my father; I never question him or purposely call any attention to myself when I'm around him. I'm queasy at the thought of riding in the car with him, but I gather Sean and pack my bottle of Pepto-Bismol in my tattered neon green bag.

"Hurry up!" Dad demands, getting into his rusted out white mustang. I'd really like to sit in the back with Sean, but because I don't want to anger him, I suck in my fear and sit up front.

We drive for about half an hour and end up in the part of town that's full of bums and prostitutes. I feel jittery inside, almost like all my senses are being pricked with needles. He drives around a corner and I see old buildings boarded with graffiti on the plywood. I'm scared and I worry at his intentions. *Why has he brought us down to this part of town?*

"What are we doing here?"

"Dummy up, I'll tell you when I'm Goddamn good and ready."

Why is he always so mean?

"Just curious—that's all."

"What the fuck, you wanna know why I brought your slutty ass down here? Because this is where you fucking belong, that's why."

I knew this was going to be something bad. I just knew it.

I stutter. "What, what are you talking about, Dad?" I swallow hard and pray I don't piss him off.

He looks at me scornfully, his eyes intense and piercing.

"You really are fucking stupid, aren't you? You're a fucking joke. Look out the fucking window, you stupid whore.

This is where you fucking belong, living on the streets with the bums."

I begin to shake and feel my head go numb.

"And those fucking braces you're wearing, the ones you talked your mother into getting for you, those are coming off tomorrow."

"But -- they're not ready to come off."

"Excuse me? Do I need to slap your cock sucker?"

"I just..."

"Now, you and that kid of yours have thirty days to get out of your mother's house. I suggest you start looking for a box big enough to house the two of you."

I feel my throat harden and my stomach turn to stone, my nerves feel on edge and my head feels thick and fuzzy. Dad speeds around the bad neighborhood and repeats how I need to live in a box, living in a box will be good for me, and it's where I belong.

"Do you understand why you need to live in a box?"

"Uh, no."

"Pfffttt, you're so damn dumb. Listen, in order to work your way up in life, you need to start at the bottom, and living in a box on the street is the bottom. Now, do you fucking understand?"

"Yeah... but...I'm moving to New York to live with Jesse," I tell him reluctantly.

He laughs, and I turn to look in the back seat at Sean. He sits with his knees up to his chin, staring wide-eyed at me. *Same kind of look Marcia always had.*

"Do you actually think that piece of shit is going to help you?"

"What do you mean? Sean and I are moving to New York in May."

"Yeah, right, that fucking...what's his name? Jesse? Isn't going to do a goddamn thing for you or for Sean. He's a piece

of shit like his fucking parents. They're shit, Holly!" He's screaming now, banging his hands on the steering wheel.
"Dad that's not nice, they're good Catholics."
"Ahh fuck me, you went and screwed a fucking Catholic, well, that says it all right there. Do they act like good Catholics? Did they help you out with Sean, fucking stupid girl!"

On the drive home, my father continues screaming and belittling me. I'm terrified, and ashamed and repulsed at myself. Staring out the window, I find a way to relieve myself of some tears, as my father pokes fun and curses at me. Sean doesn't make a sound. I take a drink of my Pepto-Bismol.

I feel confused and overwhelmed as we re-enter the townhouse. I nervously bite my lip, anticipating talking with my mother about my braces. But I won't talk to her with my father around. I don't trust him. I don't trust her either, but trust him less. Feeling completely numb, I grab Sean and head upstairs to call Jesse. I need to tell him Sean and I need to come sooner. I make the call and Jesse throws a bombshell on me. He tells me he no longer wants me to come and he's met another girl.

The news blows me away and in my mind I believe this confirms that maybe my father is right. Maybe I am just a stupid girl and Jesse and his family have never had any intention of doing the right thing in being there for Sean. Loathing my very existence, I come to understand Jesse's rejection of me. Then I think of how my father wants me and my soon to be two-year-old son to live our lives in a box. I beg Jesse to at least help take care of his son, even though at this point I believe Jesse and his parents to be just as cruel and evil as my father.

Jesse agrees to send a hundred bucks a month for child support and take Sean in the summer months. I watch Sean roll on the floor as we agree to the terms. There are no words to describe the amount of betrayal and sadness I'm feeling.

Holding Sean, I walk into the kitchen in a state of shock as I tell my mother what Jesse has decided. Then, I confront her about my braces, even though I feel uncomfortable with my father in the room.

"I'm sick of you girls taking advantage of me, that's why your father is back, to get you girls under control," she says, handing Dad a beer.

"So the fucking Catholic shows his true colors again. Jesse doesn't want you to go to New York now. Well, that doesn't surprise me. He's probably off getting some other stupid girl knocked up. Ha, ha, ha, I told you that pile of shit was a worthless fucker just like his fucking parents," Dad butts in.

"Well, really Holly, your father's right. Look what kind of parents he has. I mean the father brought over two hundred dollars in cash so you could have an abortion, and that mother of his, she's never so much as called. Holly, if you ask me your father is right, they are rotten no good piles of shit Catholics."

Of course, believe everything he says.

"Sean's better off without them. Besides, it's better this way, you never know, them being Italian they might have that mafia mentality and kick you out and keep Sean all to themselves," Mom says, handing Dad a plate of food.

"What? I don't understand. You brought him back to keep us under control?" I can feel the heartache take over my chest as I ask her this question.

"Hey, don't you even think about back talking your mother or I'll beat the shit out of you right here and now!" Dad interrupts.

"I guess I'll go move back in with Barbra then."

"You can't. Barbra and your pregnant sister are moving in together, remember? There'll be no room for you," Mom says as she picks up and holds Sean.

"Start looking for boxes young lady." Dad says, taking a swig of his cold beer and winking at me.

"I hate you. Why do you always have to be such an asshole?" *Oh shit, I didn't mean to say it out loud. How could I let that slip out, God I'm so stupid.*

Dad bolts from his chair in a fit of rage and sprints into action, ready to attack me. My keen sense of danger kicks in and I take off running toward the front door.

"You dirty fucking bitch," leaks from his tongue, just when a great force tugs at the back of my hair, pulling me down. I scream in terror. Pinning me to the floor, my father sits on my chest, pinning my wrists to the carpet with his knees. He screams obscenities, hot air spits down onto my face. I scream louder.

"Get off me, get off me." I twist and turn, heaving from his weight.

His thick hands strike my face, making a popping sound. I cry out.

"Stop, it hurts, please stop, oh God please stop."

Time seems to slow down; my head aches as though it's being devoured. The pain on my chest and face cease, the old familiar stench of evil rings in the air. I've smelt this frightening scent many times before. It's the smell of bruises; it's a metallic scent. Tears fall from my face as my body loses its hold. Mom is still holding Sean, and he screams out, a terrified, high-pitched wail. I feel the pain once again. I don't move as my face takes blows from side to side. I can sense the blotches in my skin as blood leaks from my damaged vessels. I no longer feel any desire to fight. My shivering body stops, gives up, the stench of iron boils through the atmosphere. I feel the tiny light inside close. Only emptiness survives. I'm dying, though I do not wish to die. Instead, I stare off into a blank world where I exist in an emotionless state of exile.

* * *

I've gone on to make many more mistakes in my life, including going from one hell only to find another. Jesse never made good on his agreement, and I never heard from his parents. Throughout the years I attempted to sue Jesse a couple of times, but that cost money I didn't have. I tried making new agreements with Jesse, but he went on to marry and his wife would take my calls, shooting down any requests for support or otherwise. Sean grew up, and at the age of 22 found Jesse's mother living in Florida and went to meet her. The relationship didn't last long. To this day Jesse has never met Sean, but I have no doubt he still believes himself to be a good Catholic.

I never moved into a box, the thought scared me more than anything. Instead, I found an abusive relationship that provided Sean and me a place to stay. I guess I was no different than Barbra, angry and running. I went on to marry that man, and as a result I have a lovely daughter. That marriage only lasted a couple of years.

I continued on, like many survivors of abuse, searching for love in all the wrong places. In my case, the wrong place always ended up being at my parents' door. There was never any love to get there, only abuse, but I kept going back anyway. It wasn't until my relationship with my parents was severed that I was able to heal. Barbra cut off contact with my parents many years ago. But, it was my parents who cut off contact with Marcia and me. I guess forbidding us contact was their way of still having control. Nevertheless, it was the best parenting they had ever shown.

I went on to marry again and have two more wonderful children, and it's because of all of my children that I write this book. Abuse leads to destroyed souls and empty lives. It is through writing this book that I hope to contribute in ending abuse.

*   *   *

A Healing Story…

The Torah tells me that on the tenth day of the seventh month I shall afflict my soul and do no work. For on that day God shall provide atonement and cleanse me from all my sins (Leviticus 16:29-30).

I feel and believe in order for me to continue on my healing journey I need to ask those I have wronged for forgiveness. Sitting in confines of solidarity before Yom Kippur, 2005, I begin reparations by owning the wrongs I caused those who suffered from my emaciated, under-developed, broken path. In being a wounded child and damaged adult from years of physical, emotional, verbal, spiritual, and sexual abuse, innocent people suffered as I lashed out. Today I ask for forgiveness, today I write out the wrongs I inflicted onto blameless vulnerable people that crossed my way.

Starting with my childhood memories of those I harmed:

To the two little boys I bit on the nose, I'm sorry. I don't remember what you did to irritate me, but whatever it was, you didn't deserve to be bitten on your noses. For that I am sorry, please forgive me.

To all the adults and children I had bitten, I'm sorry. My lashing out from my pain was no excuse to bite you. You didn't deserve to be hurt by a crazy little girl who wanted to hurt people the way she was being hurt. Please forgive me.

To the family pet, Tina, I'm sorry. I don't know why I chose to be mean to you, you were the one living creature that showed me comfort. You would allow me to use you as a pillow while I watched Elvis Presley movies; I'm sorry if I hurt you. I'm sorry for lashing out at you by shoving you under my bed and throwing toys at you. You deserved better, and you were the best dog a kid could ever have. Please forgive me.

To the little boy who lived up the street, I'm sorry. I didn't like you because you had a better life than me, but you didn't deserve my wrath. I'm sorry I rolled up worms in a leaf and force-fed them to you by holding you down. Please forgive me.

To the girl who lived down the hill from our apartment complex, I'm sorry. You really got under my skin, you irritated me to no end and I hated you. I'm sorry for smashing your face into the window of a parked car, and years of pulling your hair out of your head. I feel really horrible about the years of abuse I caused you. You didn't deserve that, and I'm sorry, but please understand I was in a lot of pain. Please forgive me.

To my cousin Liz. I was jealous of you, and just the fact that you were treated better by Grandma made me hate you all the more. It was not your fault that Grandma had tons of pictures of you and not of me, but that didn't stop me from being jealous of you. When Grandma finally put up pictures of my sisters and me there were always more pictures of you to overcrowd me. That was not your fault, and I'm sorry for hating you for that. I'm sorry for locking you in the basement of your house. I wanted to scare you to death, and for that I am sorry. Please forgive me.

To my cat, Petunia, I'm sorry. I treated you horribly, I turned you into a mean cat on purpose, so I could throw you at people I didn't like. My hope was for you to scratch out the eyes of those trying to harm me. You deserved a better home, not one where a girl wanted to train you to be a weapon. I'm sorry for tying you to my skateboard with my shoelaces and pushing you down the hill. I'm sorry for squeezing your little body into Barbie clothes and making you wear them for hours. I don't know what your fate was when my Dad put you in the trunk of his car, but I have no doubt you are in heaven. Please forgive me.

To my son, Sean. I am sorry I was not in the right place or time to have a child. I'm sorry you started off life being raised by an abused teen mother and a neglectful, abandoning father. I'm terribly sorry I did not know how to properly care for you and look after you; you deserved so much better and so much more. I feel absolutely horrible you had to endure pain because I didn't have the self-confidence to speak up on your behalf. I'm sorry I didn't fight for your right to be acknowledged by your father or his family. I'm sorry for causing you pain, and taking you to live with my first husband, a person we both disliked. I'm so sorry, please understand I was just a scared kid and didn't know where else to turn when Papa threw us out to live in a box on the street. You didn't deserve that, I'm so sorry. I beg for your forgiveness.

To my daughter, Shana, I am so sorry you were born to a timid, weak mother and alcoholic father. You deserved so much more than I could give you. I'm sorry for all the hard times you lived through and the neglectful father you started out your life with. I'm sorry for the pain I caused you. I am so remorseful for bringing you into the mist of my world of misery. I feel really miserable that I often lashed out at you for the pains that festered inside of me. I had no right to lash out at you, and for that I am very remorseful. You were just a child, and didn't deserve that. I beg for your forgiveness.

To my younger sister, Marcia. We had each other to rely on, but that never stopped me from taking out my anger on you. Often, during times of peace I would find you and want to bring you harm. I'm sorry for forcing you to eat hot pepper. I'm sorry for calling you nasty names, and for pushing you off the swings. I'm also sorry for bringing you pain with my wicked words when I wanted to express my hatred for you. I'm sorry for all the fights we had as kids and as adults. I should have been a better sister and understood you were in pain, too. You didn't deserve to be treated badly, and I'm sorry, please forgive me.

To my older sister, Barbra. We had some fun times sitting by my bedroom window staring out at the traffic in the middle of the night, but I hated you for not protecting me. I'm sorry for hating you, it wasn't your job to protect me, but that didn't stop me from lashing out at you. I often stole your baby-sitting money, and for that I'm sorry. I'm also sorry for tearing up your horse book; you worked hard on that book and you didn't deserve to have your little sister rip it to shreds. You lived in the same misery as I and for that I am sorry. I'm sorry for calling you nasty names and wishing you dead. I'm also sorry for all the fights we had as adults. I feel really bad that we lived a life of hell and turned against each other in the abyss of all the anger. Please forgive me.

To my husband, Steve, I'm so sorry you started out your marriage to woman who lived with constant night terrors, uncontrollable mood swings, and frantic startle responses to your presence. I'm so sorry for the pain I caused you for lashing out at you. I feel really horrible about it now that I can see what you always saw. I'm so sorry you lived in a world of frustration and helplessness because of my inabilities to admit something inside of me was not right. I apologize for hurting you by misdirecting my anger onto you, and then treating you with contempt. I really feel awful for treating you this way. You deserve to be treated like a husband. I'm sorry. Please forgive me.

To anyone else whom I may have lashed out at or who witnessed my anger, I am sorry. Please forgive me.

Finally to myself, I'm sorry. I treated myself with contempt and disparity. I treated the little girl inside with shame, guilt and anger for being a timid, feeble child that never stopped the abuse. I have shown myself more disgust and cruelty than any other person. I lived life directing hatred and revulsion within, and I hated my adult self for being weak and frail. I'm sorry; I apologize to myself for not trusting me, and for not feeling worthy. Please forgive me.

I forgive myself for harming me. I forgive myself for not being able to protect myself, and I forgive myself for not trusting in myself. I free myself from the burden of self-destruction, self-torture, and self-blame. I forgive Me.

"It's okay to cry over spilled milk."

Printed in the United States
79982LV00003B/148